THREE BOWLS

SILENCE

THREE BOWLS

Vegetarian Recipes from an American Zen Buddhist Monastery

SEPPO ED FARREY

Head Chef of Dai Bosatsu Zendo

with

MYOCHI NANCY O'HARA

Foreword and Calligraphy by

EIDO T. SHIMANO ROSHI

Houghton Mifflin Company
Boston   New York
2000

For information about permission to reproduce selections from this book, write to Permissions, Houghton Mifflin Company, 215 Park Avenue South, New York, New York 10003.

Visit our Web site: www.hmco.com/trade.

Library of Congress Cataloging-in-Publication Data
Farrey, Seppo Ed.
Three bowls : vegetarian recipes from an American Zen Buddhist monastery /
    Seppo Ed Farrey, with Myochi Nancy O'Hara ; foreword and calligraphy by
    Eido T. Shimano Roshi.
    p. cm.
    ISBN 0-395-97707-X
    1. Vegetarian cookery. I. O'Hara, Myochi Nancy. II. Dai Bosatsu Zendo
    Monastery. III. Title.
    TX837.F29 2000
    641.5'636 — dc21   00-026916

Book design by Anne Chalmers
Typefaces: Linotype Hell Electra, Visigoth, Universe Condensed, Futura Condensed

Printed in United States of America
QUM 10 9 8 7 6 5 4 3 2 1

CONTENTS

JOYOUS MIND

ACKNOWLEDGMENTS

IT GIVES ME GREAT PLEASURE TO BE ABLE TO acknowledge the many people who have influenced my cooking and this book. Influence comes from so many places, from restaurant menus, the authors of hundreds of cookbooks, friends who are professional chefs, and the many people who have worked in the tenzo at Dai Bosatsu Zendo with me. I would like to thank:

First and foremost, Eido Roshi, for his karma to come to America and found Dai Bosatsu Zendo, for without him the monastery would not exist, and without a monastery or a sangha to cook for, *Three Bowls* would never have been written; also for his unwavering commitment to the dharma, for his powerful enigmatic teachings, and, with my palms together and a deep bow for his generosity, for his exquisite calligraphy and willingness to write the foreword.

Aiho Yasuko Shimano, the director of New York Zendo Shobo-ji and the wife of Eido Roshi, for the opportunity to assist and watch as she magically prepared and quietly served elegant spreads of traditional Japanese delicacies to hundreds of people.

Myochi Nancy O'Hara, for without her persistent cajoling and encouragement, I would have never embarked on this project, for leading me by the hand through the initial stages of writing the book, for proofreading my early writing and for whipping my rusty skills back into shape, for testing many of the recipes in her home kitchen to make certain they would work, and for the close friendship formed as a result of working side by side on this book for two and a half years.

Sarah Jane Freymann, our literary agent, who helped focus our ideas into a manuscript that got more attention than I ever imagined, and for her wonderful "agenting."

Rux Martin, our editor, with whom I felt an instant connection and rapport, for her warmth, advice, blind faith in me, and clear vision of *Three Bowls*.

The residents and extended sangha of Dai Bosatsu Zendo and Shobo-ji for their support, encouragement, and criticism.

My mother and father, Shirley Farrey and Edward A. Farrey, for their unconditional love and support, no matter what endeavor I undertake or which path I tread. Special thanks to my mother for teaching me kitchen and cooking basics from an early age.

My aunt, Nancy Farrey, who gave me my first hardcover cookbook, *The Way to Cook* by Julia Child, which impressed me and which I read from cover to cover. It opened the door to my love of food and cooking.

Richard Pierce and Patrick Donnelly of the Whole Foods Project in New York City for my very first vegetarian cooking classes and for introducing me to whole-foods cuisine.

Judy Kaestner, for her vegetarian whole-foods cooking savvy, which she enthusiastically shares with me, and for erratic hours on the phone lost in food talk.

All the chefs and owners I have worked with in restaurants over the last twenty years, who have educated me in many ways.

Chisho Fusaye Maas, for first planting the seed of this book in my mind.

Chika Bettina Vitell, for her support and encouragement in this endeavor, and for allowing me to include an adapted version of her recipe for Szechuan Green Beans and Soba.

Entsu Scott Rosecrans, our resident breadmaster, for allowing me to adapt some of his recipes, for acting as my baking consultant, and for creating and testing the yeast breads.

Seiko Susan Morningstar, for inspiring some of my creations, and for her scrupulous and sober honesty.

Seigan Edwin Glassing, who was kind enough to taste-test many recipes, and for his perseverance through the "muffin-mania" phase of this cookbook.

All of my generous assistants, who have become good friends as well: Jigen Delys Molis Young, Judith Molis, Angela Mortensen, and Genno Linda King. And those who have come and gone, but who have forever left an impact on my tenzo practice and my cooking: Sangen Akihiro Tanaka, Yuko Himada, and Zensan Hiromi Suzuki.

My dear friends, for their support and encouragement through this project and through my life's journey: Juan Urosa, for teaching me the basics of authentic Mexican cooking, and for his unconditional love and friendship; Dunja Lingwood, for instilling a new and very generous concept of heart and spirit in my practice; Raymond Lamb, whose pure heart, unconditional love, and lasting friendship have taught me generosity, faith, and gratitude for life itself; and Steve Baeck, for introducing me to the idea of eating food from foreign lands as well as to the food itself.

Steven Petusevsky, who generously allowed me to use his recipe for Garden Brown Sauce.

My friends at www.theKitchenLink.com, who have supported me through this project; most notably Betsy Couch; Sarah Phillips, for her generous and savvy advice; Suzanne Geffre, for allowing me to adapt her recipe for Semolina Rolls; Julie Padwick, for permitting adaptation of her Tahini Butternut Squash recipe; and my many friends at TKL chat.

— Seppo Ed Farrey

I'D LIKE TO EXPRESS MY GRATITUDE TO Eido Shimano Roshi for coming to this country and establishing an authentic Rinzai Zen practice that saved and then enriched my life. Without him, and without his able partner, Aiho Yasuko Shimano, many things would not have happened here in the West, including this book. And to Boun Nancy Berg, who first introduced me to Dai Bosatsu Zendo and the practice of Zen meditation, I am eternally grateful.

It has been a joy and an honor working with Seppo in his tenzo and on this project. Sarah Jane Freymann's vision and helpful guidance were crucial. We couldn't have had a better editor than Rux Martin. Without being a Zen practitioner, she understands it in her bones — a true Zen student. My special thanks to Seigan Ed Glassing for his expert commentaries and friendship. I am thankful to the monks, nuns, residents, friends, and extended sangha of Dai Bosatsu Zendo. I salute you and bow to you all in gratitude for your encouragement and your practice. Together, you make it all work. Thank you and *gassho*.

—Myochi Nancy O'Hara

FOREWORD

EVERY DAY AT OUR MONASTERY, AFTER THE MORNING AND midday meals, we chant a verse known as the Five Reflections.

First, let us reflect on our own work and the effort of those who brought us this food.
Second, let us be aware of the quality of our deeds as we receive this meal.
Third, what is most essential is the practice of mindfulness, which helps us transcend greed, anger, and delusion.
Fourth, we appreciate this food, which sustains the good health of our body and mind.
Fifth, in order to continue our practice for all beings, we accept this offering.

A few words in *The Five Reflections* glitter like diamonds: *reflect on our own work; the quality of our deeds; the practice of mindfulness; appreciate this food; practice for all beings;* and most important, *the effort of those who brought us this food.* In the monastery, the person who prepares the food is called the *tenzo.* The tenzo does invisible work, planning and shopping to create tangible food for others.

The thirteenth-century Japanese Zen master Dogen Zenji said in *Instructions to a Tenzo* that there are three important minds a tenzo should have: Joyful Mind, Great Mind, and Mature Mind. Cooking is not only the preparation of food but a practice of spirituality. A practice of spirituality means not wasting even the stem of a vegetable. It involves economy of movement, punctuality, and beauty of presentation. These are the elements that make our lives spiritually rich. We can be rich even without a dollar. We can be destitute with a fortune. If you are content, you are already the richest person in the world. *Three Bowls* is not merely a cookbook but a spiritual guide for us all.

—Eido T. Shimano Roshi
Dai Bosatsu Zendo, Catskill Mountains
December 1, 1999

INTRODUCTION

MY COOKING BEGINS EACH DAY AT 6:35 A.M., WHEN I enter the cold, dark monastery kitchen directly after our morning chanting service in the dharma hall. The west wall of the kitchen is a bank of windows from end to end. Later in the day, the windows will be my saviors from the heat of the kitchen, but for now, the predawn air carries a chill. I hustle out of my robes and into my work clothes and lace up my shoes. My brain begins to whir with the details of exactly what needs to be executed, and in which order.

The abbot of the monastery, Eido Roshi, and the monks are still in the main hall doing zazen (sitting meditation), and they will stay there until I strike the meal gong. It's crucial that I call them precisely at 7:15 A.M. for breakfast and 1:00 P.M. for lunch. As in any family, we each have a schedule to keep. The residents of the monastery follow a stringent routine, and if I fall behind, I delay everyone else. Preparing breakfast is a familiar practice: the same each morning, yet slightly different — a peaceful way to start the day.

I am the head chef, or tenzo, at Dai Bosatsu Zendo, a traditional Rinzai Zen Buddhist monastery in a remote forest high in the Catskill Mountains. Each day, I am responsible for preparing the meals for the twelve to twenty-four monks and laypersons who live here, as well as up to seventy visitors who come to the monastery for retreats.

In keeping with the tenets of Buddhism, all of the meals served at Dai Bosatsu are entirely vegetarian. The food must be substantial enough to sustain the monks through their three-hour work shifts — there is no snacking. During sesshin, an intensive seven-day silent meditation retreat, the fare must carry the residents and guests through long hours of intense meditation, so it is particularly important that the meals be well-balanced, nourishing, and hearty.

Breakfast and lunch are formal meals that follow rituals established in traditional Zen monasteries, and are served and eaten in silence. Each diner gets three bowls — a large bowl, a medium bowl, and a small bowl — and chopsticks. The largest bowl contains the base of the meal, usually a grain or noodle dish, such as Basmati Rice with Raisins and Walnuts or Herbed Sesame Polenta with Roasted Vegetables. The middle bowl is usually filled with a stew, such as Almond Thai Curry. A vegetable dish like Asparagus with Lime and Tamari, or occasionally a salad, rounds out the meal in the third and smallest bowl. The silence allows us to focus solely on what we are eating, be grateful for our food, and reflect on all those who are responsible for it: farmers and workers in the fields, truckers, grocery store employees, and finally, the tenzos who have prepared it.

Supper is a casual meal in the residents' lounge. Usually, it's leftovers supplemented by a few basics, such as bread, cheese, and nut butters. During sesshin, when more sustenance is needed, supper is served formally. Traditionally, it consists of a big crock of hearty soup, such as Butternut–Black Bean Soup or Cilantro-Lemon Vegetable Soup, nourishing homemade bread served with a savory spread, such as Lentil-Walnut Pâté or Tahini Applesauce Spread, and a tossed green salad served with a dressing, such as Avocado-Wasabi Dressing or Strawberry-Cilantro Dressing.

Although the manner of serving is traditionally Japanese, the food itself is eclectic, inspired by the many visiting Japanese monks who have taught me their specialties, as well as by visiting professional chefs and monastery residents and guests from around the world who have assisted me in the kitchen as part of their work practice. The result is global vegetarian cooking, which brings together unlikely ingredients from different cultures in harmonious combinations. I try to keep the food as healthful as possible, without letting it become too boring or repetitive. Many of the recipes in this book are representative of "whole-foods" cooking, and a number are vegan and low-fat. Others are more extravagant options that are served for celebration dinners, such as Sesame Crepes with Portobello Mushrooms in Port Cream Sauce, Savory Whipped Sweet Potatoes with Ribbons of Collard Greens, and Coconut-Pecan Carrot Cake with Orange–Cream Cheese Frosting. People are occasionally surprised to find some of these dishes at a Zen monastery. I think it's best not to limit yourself with ideas about what "should" or "shouldn't" be served — Zen, after all, is paradoxical by nature.

As with all cooks, my repertoire is dictated by the needs of the people I cook for — their preferences, eccentricities, and special diets — so in that respect, cooking for the residents is no different from cooking for any family. And, like most cooks, I try to rise to the daily challenge of keeping meals interesting while staying within a budget and on a tight schedule. Our monastery is located twenty miles from the nearest small town and even farther from any major source of food supplies, so I plan ahead and rely on a well-stocked pantry, often making do without out-of-season produce.

Some of my most delectable dishes have been born from leftovers. Sweet Potato–Walnut Burritos were devised to use up sweet potatoes and lentils from a previous meal. Beet Raita with Dill, Lime, and Honey was the result of not having cucumbers. Coconut Corn Bread, which has become a favorite, evolved from a recipe that originally called for jalapeños, not coconut. Necessity may have mothered invention, but in my kitchen, invention often takes on a life of its own.

The tenzo routine, like the routine of daily meditation, has gradually become a spiritual practice, providing me with a valuable opportunity to serve and nurture others. The right qualities of heart and mind in cooking are just as important as a stove or a knife.

Many of the dishes in this book get better if allowed "to sit in themselves." Their flavors meld and mature. And the more we sit and do zazen, the more we fuse with the universe and the more we mature on many levels, in both apparent and imperceptible ways.

— Seppo Ed Farrey

THAT I WOULD LEARN ABOUT MEDITATION IN A ZEN
Buddhist monastery was not a surprise. The surprise
was what I learned from the monks about spiritual
enrichment when we weren't doing zazen. I was
first introduced to Dai Bosatsu Zendo in 1988, when
I attended a weekend retreat. My life hasn't been
the same since.

Chanting, drinking tea, eating meals, working
assigned jobs — fully engaged in each moment,
wasting nothing, sharing unconditionally — the
monks taught me to value every precious moment.
They taught me that while time set aside for prayer
and meditation is critical, the same attitudes honed
in meditation must be brought to every activity and
every moment and encounter of every day, otherwise the time spent sitting and meditating is for
nothing. Reading Buddhist texts brings only partial
understanding. In order to fully grasp the meaning
of life, we must experience it. Sitting still and concentrating on our breath, practicing our work with
total concentration, eating with awareness — everything must be done with mindfulness.

Eating with the monks that first weekend, I
learned as much, or perhaps more, about the practice of being in each moment than I learned
through sitting zazen. The meals are taken in
silence. Before and after, prayers are chanted to give
thanks. The food is passed down each table, and no
one begins eating until everyone is served. At the
end, after everyone has washed the bowls at the

table and wrapped them in cotton cloths, the group
files out of the dining room. I quickly noticed that if
my mind strayed, I'd either miss out on what was
being served or I'd be left with a bowl of food,
unable to finish it and with no place to hide it. This
mealtime ritual taught me to pay attention. It taught
me to take only as much as I thought I could eat
and no more. It taught me to acknowledge that I
can learn from others as I strive to master the Zen
art of eating. And it taught me to appreciate the
silence, to have reverence for the food, to concentrate on what was in front of me, and to *just eat*.

Like me, most of the group was there for the first
time, and we struggled together to fit into the rituals
of the monastery. We fumbled our way through that
first silent meal, chuckling under our breath at our
awkward manners as we ate oatmeal with chopsticks
and tried to wash our bowls without too much mess
or noise. We all made it, and by the end of the weekend we were fairly adept at this new way of eating.
What lingered was the deliciousness of the food. It
was as though we were learning to eat and to savor
what we were eating for the first time.

Since then, I've continued to retreat to Dai Bosatsu Zendo. After many trips and one five-month stay,
I have learned to pay attention to what I eat, wherever I eat. Over the past few years, I've also had the
privilege of conducting weekend retreats at the
monastery and introducing others to Zen practice.
Prior to arriving there, many people express anxiety

about what the food will be like. Those who are not accustomed to eating vegetarian fare are most keenly anxious. But the lusciousness of the meals not only calms their fears but makes most people want to change their eating habits. At the very least, they want to take some of the recipes home with them. I am thrilled to finally have this book to offer them, and to share Seppo's cooking with the rest of the world.

Like all good cooks, Seppo uses what he has and invents as he goes along. As you begin to cook, try to adopt the same attitude: be reverential, be creative, be thankful, take some risks. Learn from others and then experiment for yourself. Take the time to appreciate what you prepare.

—Myochi Nancy O'Hara

PURIFY

MINDFUL COOKING

Before selecting the recipes you wish to prepare, consider those you will be feeding and what they might enjoy. Then bring all your attention to the food. Food lovingly and mindfully prepared tastes better and satisfies longer.

FIRST. Consider the time you have allotted to cook and wisely choose the recipes you wish to prepare, with your time constraints in mind. Rushing only serves to undermine mindfulness.

SECOND. Before you begin, check to make sure you have on hand all the needed ingredients or workable substitutes.

THIRD. Wash, chop, sift, and stir. Think only of washing, chopping, sifting, and stirring. Breathe and be mindful of each slice of the knife, of each swirl of the spoon, of the magical process of cooking.

FOURTH. Before throwing anything away, consider whether it might have a use. For example, save vegetable remains to make soup stock or use them as compost to feed your garden.

FIFTH. Keep it simple. Relax and enjoy the process of cooking, and the miracles that are born from your efforts. Sometimes we get so carried away that we can't stop, and with all good intentions, we make more food than anyone could possibly eat at one sitting. If you want to make four or five or six different dishes for one meal, remind yourself that three are plenty.

FORMAL BREAKFAST IS SERVED PRECISELY AT 7:15 A.M. AND IS EATEN IN robes and in silence. It usually consists of a hearty, nourishing porridge, condiments, orange juice, and a large platter of fresh seasonal fruit. The porridge is a wonderfully warming way to begin the day on this cold mountaintop, and it provides a nutritionally sound base for the day, energizing us for the long work period ahead.

It usually consists of a grain that has been slowly cooked and stirred, such as Cream of Quinoa, or sometimes a combination of grains; Hearty Five-Grain Porridge, for example, is made from barley, bulgur, rice, millet, and oats. The most traditional Zen monastery breakfast, Rice Porridge, is our favorite.

Unlike most American hot cereals, which are sweetened and served with milk, this porridge is a vehicle for salty and spicy condiments. Though we eat it almost every day, it is anything but boring. The array of accompaniments — tamari, scallions, nori, sesame seeds, and Korean kimchee, to name a few — keep it interesting, and I usually provide five or six different choices for diners. In this simple manner, our breakfast varies each morning while remaining constant.

Since I have only 40 minutes after the morning chanting service to prepare breakfast, it's necessary to do quite a bit of preparation the day before. I rinse the rice, bring it to a quick boil, and let it sit covered overnight to absorb water. My assistant and I also prepare the condiments, place them in serving bowls (refrigerating them if necessary), and select and wash the fruit. In the morning, we finish cooking the porridge, slice the fruit and arrange it on the serving platter, prepare coffee and tea, sometimes boil eggs, and get everything out to the table by 7:15. It's always a challenge.

An informal brunch is served every rest-day morning (usually Mondays) and also at the close of sesshin, an intense seven-day silent retreat. Informal meals are served buffet style without the traditional three bowls or robes. Aside from the food, the best part of these meals is the conversation.

These informal meals give me a liberating perspective and start my creative juices flowing. I can serve more than three dishes and prepare food that won't be eaten with chopsticks, like Banana Pecan Waffles and Oatmeal Pancakes. Although these informal brunches may seem more festive and celebratory, the mindfulness of the formal breakfasts makes them the true treasures of our practice.

— Seppo

"The essence of Zen is so simple that it can be described in one short word:
JUST. Just! Just this! This right here, right now."

— Eido Roshi

Rice Porridge with Condiments

This is a meal that many of our regular guests eagerly anticipate when they visit. We can't take credit for this recipe: rice porridge, known as *okayu* in Japan, has been the traditional breakfast in Zen temples for centuries. Visitors who have eaten at Zen Buddhist monasteries in Japan tell us that *okayu* is more appropriately called "rice water," since it stretches the precious ingredients as far as possible. Our porridge, in contrast, is much more substantial, more like a thick, sumptuous soup. Although it is traditionally made with white rice, I prefer to use short-grain brown rice. You can make it with any variety you like.

MAKES 4 SERVINGS

1¼ cups short-grain brown rice, rinsed well and drained
  Condiments (pages 6–8)

1. The night before you plan to serve the porridge, bring 6 cups water to a boil in a medium saucepan. Add the rice, return to a rolling boil, cover, and remove from the heat. Let stand covered at room temperature overnight. (Alternatively, to cook the porridge the same day, bring 6 cups water to a boil and add the rice. Reduce the heat to very low, cover, and simmer for about 1½ hours, stirring a few times during the final ½ hour.)

2. In the morning, place the covered pot over medium-high heat and cook, stirring occasionally. If the mixture seems dry, add a small amount of hot water — just enough to give it a slightly soupy consistency. Continue cooking, stirring occasionally, until the porridge is creamy, adding hot water a little at a time, if necessary. When the rice has reached the desired consistency and is heated through, serve with a selection of the condiments.

NOTE: By starting the porridge and preparing the condiments the night before, as I do, you can easily fit this breakfast into a "rise-and-run" lifestyle.

You may want to soak and cook a small handful of dried beans to toss into the finished rice porridge. (I use black, pinto, or adzuki beans.) Leftover cooked greens, such as kale or spinach, also make a tasty addition.

Spicy and Salty Condiments

Some of these condiments are served only occasionally, while others are offered practically every morning.

BASIC CONDIMENTS

Tamari

Sesame seeds, toasted

Nori (see below), cut into small pieces

Scallions, thinly sliced (see page 45)

Korean kimchee

OTHER CONDIMENTS

Hard-boiled eggs, crumbled by hand

Cooked beans

Cooked greens

Sliced shiitake mushrooms

Umeboshi plums

Pickled daikon *(takuan)*, thinly sliced

TO TOAST NUTS, WHEAT GERM, COCONUT, SEEDS, OR SPICES: Toasting adds richness and depth to all these condiments. Place a heavy-bottomed dry skillet over medium-low heat. Add the ingredient and heat, stirring constantly, until it becomes fragrant and golden brown, 1 to 5 minutes, depending on what you're toasting. Immediately pour the condiment out of the pan and into a small bowl to stop the cooking process. It's best to keep a small amount of the untoasted ingredient by the stovetop so you don't overcook or burn the condiment, since subtle changes in color can be difficult to detect.

TO PREPARE NORI: A standard sheet of nori is 7 x 8 inches. Several sheets of nori can be cut at once. With the short side toward you, cut with scissors along the long side, making 8 equal strips, about 1 inch wide. Stack the strips and cut through them every ½ inch, forming approximately ½-x-1-inch pieces.

TO HARD-BOIL AN EGG: I adapted this method from Julia Child, and it never fails to produce hard-boiled eggs that are easy to peel. Bring enough water to cover the eggs by 1 inch to a boil in a medium saucepan. Using a ladle, gently lower the desired number of eggs into the boiling water. Cook for 9 minutes for a slightly soft center or 10 minutes for a firmer center. (These times are accurate for up to 20 eggs in one pot.) Immediately remove the eggs from the boiling water (keep the water boiling) and place in a bath of very cold water under a running faucet for 2 minutes. Gently lower the eggs back into the boiling water for 10 seconds. Return the eggs to the cold water bath, gently cracking them, for at least 2 minutes. Keeping the eggs in the cold water bath longer is fine but will cool the inside of the egg. The first chilling makes the whites shrink from the shells, while plunging the eggs into boiling water a second time expands the shell and allows it to pull away from the egg. Peel the eggs under a stream of cold running water or in the cold water bath.

Sweet and Creamy Condiments

An Americanized version of Rice Porridge can be made by serving it with sweet condiments.

Maple syrup or honey

Milk, soy milk, rice milk, or yogurt

Ground cinnamon

Raisins or other dried fruits

Walnuts or peanuts, toasted (see page 6)

Wheat germ, toasted (see page 6)

Coconut, toasted (see page 6)

Sesame or sunflower seeds, toasted (see page 6)

NOTE: Instead of adding cinnamon to an entire pot of hot cereal, I keep it in a saltshaker to offer to our guests. It's easy to sprinkle and far nicer than putting a commercial spice container on the table.

HOW TO CRACK A HARD-BOILED EGG

During one of Roshi's formal talks, we were given a lesson in the matter of cracking a hard-boiled egg Zen style. In his inimitable fashion, Roshi demonstrated how most of us had cracked the shell of our egg that morning at breakfast, and then how a Rinzai Zen student should crack an egg. Not as we had done, with multiple taps on the table, but with one loud thump. Pierce the silence and be done with it.

Next morning what a difference. Crack. Pow. Bang. And then quiet. No tentative taps. A tap sufficient to crack the egg, contrasting with the silence and somehow not disturbing it. Simple. Elegant. Brisk. Determined. The Rinzai approach to cracking an egg.

— Myochi

Hearty Five-Grain Porridge

This substantial cereal is a flavorful and healthy way to start the day. I serve it throughout the year, though it's especially wonderful on a cold winter morning. Serve with sweet or salty condiments — or whatever you usually enjoy on your hot cereal. This porridge takes only slightly longer than oatmeal if you start it the night before.

MAKES 6 TO 8 SERVINGS

¾ cup bulgur, rinsed well and drained
½ cup short-grain brown rice, rinsed well and drained
½ cup millet, rinsed well and drained
⅓ cup barley, rinsed well and drained
½ cup old-fashioned rolled oats
1¼ teaspoons sea salt
1 teaspoon vanilla extract (if using Sweet and Creamy Condiments)

Spicy and Salty Condiments (page 6)
or Sweet and Creamy Condiments (page 8)

1. The night before you plan to serve the porridge, bring 6½ cups water to a boil in a large saucepan. Add the bulgur, brown rice, millet, and barley, return to a rolling boil, cover, and remove from the heat. Let stand covered at room temperature overnight. (Alternatively, to cook the porridge the same day, bring 6½ cups water to a boil in a large saucepan and add the bulgur, brown rice, millet, and barley. Reduce the heat to very low, cover, and simmer for about 1 hour, stirring a few times during the last 20 minutes. Add 2 cups boiling water, the oats, salt, and vanilla, if using. Bring to a boil, reduce the heat to very low, cover, and simmer for about 20 minutes more, stirring occasionally, or until the grains are tender.)

2. In the morning, whisk 3½ cups boiling water into the grain mixture. Stir in the oats and salt, cover, and bring to a boil, stirring occasionally to prevent the grains from sticking to the bottom of the pan. Reduce the heat to very low and simmer, stirring occasionally, until the porridge thickens and the grains are tender, 15 to 20 minutes. Stir in the vanilla, if using. Serve hot with condiments.

Three-Grain Cereal

This cereal is a light, smooth, and naturally creamy combination of grains. It's more delicate than Hearty Five-Grain Porridge (page 10), but very nutritious nonetheless.

MAKES 2 TO 4 SERVINGS

½ cup quinoa, rinsed well and drained
⅓ cup millet, rinsed well and drained
¾ teaspoon sea salt
¼ cup farina (Cream of Wheat)

   Sweet and Creamy Condiments (page 8)

1. The night before you plan to serve the cereal, bring 4 cups water to a boil in a medium saucepan. Add the quinoa and millet, return to a rolling boil, cover, and remove from the heat. Let stand covered at room temperature overnight. (Alternatively, to cook the cereal the same day, bring 4 cups water to a boil in a medium saucepan and add the quinoa, millet, farina, and salt. Return to a boil, reduce the heat to very low, cover, and simmer for about 20 minutes, stirring occasionally, until all the water has been absorbed. Add 1 cup boiling water and continue to simmer, stirring occasionally, for 10 to 15 minutes, until the cereal reaches the desired consistency.)

2. In the morning, whisk 1 cup boiling water and the salt into the cereal and bring to a boil. Reduce the heat to very low and whisk in the farina, stirring constantly for 1 minute. Cover and simmer, stirring occasionally, until thickened, 2 to 10 minutes more. Serve hot with your favorite condiments.

JIHATSU

For the Zen ritual of eating, we are all given our own set of three nesting bowls, neatly wrapped in a simple square of brown cotton cloth. These wrapped bowls are called jihatsu sets. *Ji* means "hold"; *hatsu* means "bowl." On top of the wrapped Jihatsu bowls sits another piece of twice-folded cloth that covers the bowls squarely. This folded cloth neatens the appearance of all the sets of bowls and covers a four-by-six-inch index card that contains the meal chants. It also covers the white cleaning cloth we use to dry our bowls, which can get quite dirty after a few meals.

We file into the dining room in the same order that we sit in the zendo and stand with bowls in hand. The tenzo rings the meal gong, loud-soft, loud-soft, until we are all in place. Then the head monk of the zendo rings his bell, and we all sit awaiting the next signal. In unison we begin to unwrap our bowls, placing our cover cloths and wiping cloths on our laps. Taking the chopsticks from their cover, we set them on the table at an angle, pointed ends overhanging the edge, with the large bowl on the left, the medium bowl in the center, and the small bowl on the right next to the chopsticks.

The food is presented in large serving bowls that we slide down the table on place mats. In turn, we each take hold of the mat with one hand, as the person opposite does the same, and drag it so that it is directly in front of us. With palms together in front of our hearts, we signal that we'd like some of what is being passed and take only as much as we can eat, or we bow our heads to decline. After the last bowl has been passed, we pull an offering board down the table in the same way, and with our chop-sticks we each remove the equivalent of seven grains of rice and place them on the board.

As we serve ourselves, we chant *Kanzeon*, a joyous chant that gives thanks and proclaims our true nature to be eternal, joyous, selfless, and pure. Or we chant *Namu Dai Bosa*, a simpler chant to memorize, which means gratitude. It's a lot to remember. Hands together means yes, bowing or nodding the head means no. Don't begin until the signal is given, stop when the signal is given, begin again, stop again, bow, nod, chant. Whew!

One of the monks claps the clappers, and we chant some more. Clappers end it, and then finally we eat!

The tea water arrives. This is for cleanup. Look at the others, do what they do. But we were told not to look around. I'll just move my eyes to glance at the monk a few people across to my left. See what he does. Pour water in big bowl. Wash small bowl in big bowl and dry. Pour water into medium bowl, wash big bowl in medium bowl. Oops, first wash chopsticks and put back in their cloth sleeve and place on table. Now pour water back into big bowl. Wash and dry medium bowl in big bowl, stack with small bowl. Drink remaining tea water in big bowl or wait for receptacle and dump water. Dry big bowl. Stack all three bowls, quietly. Wrap in cloth. Place the chopsticks on top, then the cleaning cloth, then the cover cloth. Wipe the table with the cleaning rag when it makes its way to you. When the person opposite is done, place the wrapped bowls directly in front of you on table. Wait for the signal. Chant along.

Rise, wait for the signal, turn and file out of the dining room, bowls in hand, back to the zendo. Bow to each other when the signal is given. Return the bowls behind your cushion. Kneel on the cushion. Rise again when signaled. File out of the zendo. Proceed to the next event.

What an ordeal! What a meal! What a challenge! What does it all mean? I couldn't wait to do it again.

— Myochi

Oatmeal with Sweet Potato and Apricots

Stirring grated sweet potato and dried apricots into oatmeal produces an earthy sweetness with a heartier taste than fruit alone would contribute. This is a tasty and different way to start the morning.

MAKES 2 TO 4 SERVINGS

2 cups old-fashioned rolled oats
1 medium sweet potato, peeled and grated (about 3 cups)
4 dried apricots, chopped
¾ teaspoon sea salt
1 teaspoon vanilla extract

Sweet and Creamy Condiments (page 8)

Bring 5½ cups water to a boil in a large saucepan. Stir in the oats, sweet potato, apricots, and salt and return to a boil. Reduce the heat to very low, cover, and simmer, stirring occasionally, until the oats are tender and the sweet potato is cooked, about 20 minutes. Stir in the vanilla. Serve with the condiments.

VARIATIONS

Basic Oatmeal

When guests sample my oatmeal, they always wonder why it is so much better than the oatmeal they make at home. The answer is simple. I don't use quick-cooking or packaged name-brand oatmeal. I use rolled oats that can be found in any natural food store in the bulk bins. Surprisingly, even organic oatmeal is far less expensive than any variety purchased from your local supermarket.

Follow the directions for Oatmeal with Sweet Potato and Apricots, omitting the sweet potato and apricots and reducing the amount of water to 5 cups. The vanilla is optional.

Cinnamon Apple Oatmeal

I use unsweetened applesauce when I'm in a hurry, but fresh apples can be peeled, grated, and used instead.

Follow the directions for Basic Oatmeal. After 15 minutes of cooking, just before it is done, mix in 1 cup unsweetened applesauce or 1 peeled, grated apple, 1 teaspoon ground cinnamon, and 1 teaspoon vanilla.

OATMEAL WITH CHOPSTICKS

Why didn't I ask for a spoon? I've eaten in enough Chinese restaurants to be able to wield a set of chopsticks, so my pride kept me from asking for one. But I didn't think the monastery would serve something that would be so hard to eat. I decide to do my best, and I must finish everything because soon I'll have to wash and rewrap my bowls. Everyone seems to be eating so fast! I'll never be done in time. Why do they eat so quickly? I thought this practice was about mindfulness. How can I be mindful if I'm racing to get the food down?

I don't remember which bowl to wash first. How much water should I take? Oh my God, seconds already. I haven't even finished firsts. Better pay attention here.

— Myochi

Cream of Quinoa

Among the residents, this cereal has become known as "cream of wah." With more protein, higher levels of unsaturated fats, and lower carbohydrate values than most grains, quinoa provides a rich and balanced source of many vital nutrients. For the most part, cream of quinoa can cook on its own while you prepare yourself for the day ahead. The flavor is similar to cream of wheat, but with a hint of nuttiness.

MAKES 2 TO 4 SERVINGS

1 cup quinoa, rinsed well and drained

½ teaspoon sea salt

Sweet and Creamy Condiments (page 8)

Bring 4 cups water and the quinoa to a boil in a medium saucepan. Reduce the heat to very low, cover, and cook until thickened, about 30 minutes. Stir in the salt. Serve hot with your favorite condiments.

A monk said to the Chinese Zen master Joshu, "I am a beginner. Will you please teach me?"

Joshu asked him, "Have you had breakfast?"

The monk replied, "Yes, I have."

Joshu responded, "Then wash your bowl."

With this, the monk gained insight.

— From *The Gateless Gate*, translated by Eido Roshi

Oatmeal Pancakes

Our resident breadmaster, Entsu Scott Rosecrans, developed these pancakes. I perfected them, following my own intuition, and the result is a bit of my whimsy tossed into Entsu's pancakes. We all agree that they're wonderful. Serve with maple syrup, Sautéed Gingered Apples (page 22), or Double-Berry Poached Pears (page 204).

MAKES ABOUT 10 PANCAKES

1¼ cups milk, soy milk, or rice milk
1 cup old-fashioned rolled oats
½ cup whole wheat pastry flour or unbleached white flour
1 tablespoon plus 1 teaspoon baking powder
½ teaspoon sea salt
2 large eggs
4 tablespoons (½ stick) unsalted butter, melted, or unsweetened applesauce
1 tablespoon plus 1 teaspoon honey
1 teaspoon vanilla extract

1. Bring 1 cup of the milk to a boil in a small saucepan. Add the oats, reduce the heat to very low, cover, and simmer for 5 minutes. Remove from the heat, uncover, stir, and let stand, stirring a few times, until most of the milk is absorbed, about 15 minutes.

2. Combine the flour, baking powder, and salt in a large bowl. Whisk together the eggs, remaining ¼ cup milk, butter or applesauce, honey, and vanilla in a small bowl. Add to the dry ingredients along with the oat mixture and stir just until moistened.

3. Lightly coat a skillet with spray, oil, or butter and preheat over medium heat. Pour ¼ cup batter into the pan, spread it a bit with the side of a spatula or measuring cup, and cook until bubbles form on top and the underside is nicely browned, 1½ to 2 minutes. Flip the pancake over, press gently with the back of a spatula to flatten, and cook until the other side is browned, about 1 minute. Continue until all the batter is used. The finished pancakes can be kept warm in a 150°F oven. For crisper pancakes, place on a baking sheet; for softer pancakes, cover the baking sheet with foil. Serve hot.

NOTE: You can substitute an equal amount of whole wheat flour for the whole wheat pastry flour.

Banana Pecan Waffles

Serve these tender waffles with Fruit Compote (page 23), Sautéed Gingered Apples (page 22), or Double-Berry Poached Pears (page 204). You can also reduce the pear-poaching liquid to a syrupy sauce and serve it with the waffles along with crème fraîche or sour cream. Or serve the waffles with the traditional butter and maple syrup.

MAKES ABOUT 18 WAFFLES

2 cups whole wheat pastry flour or unbleached white flour

1 cup pecans or walnuts, toasted (see page 6) and finely chopped

2 teaspoons baking powder

1½ teaspoons baking soda

½ teaspoon sea salt

1¾ cups low-fat buttermilk

¾ cup mashed ripe banana

3 large eggs, separated

¼ cup honey

3 tablespoons unsalted butter, melted, or unsweetened applesauce

1 teaspoon vanilla extract

1. Lightly coat a waffle iron with spray, oil, or butter and plug it in to preheat.

2. Combine the flour, pecans or walnuts, baking powder, baking soda, and salt thoroughly in a large bowl. Whisk together the buttermilk, bananas, egg yolks, honey, butter or applesauce, and vanilla in a medium bowl. Add the wet ingredients to the dry ingredients and mix just until evenly blended.

3. Beat the egg whites until stiff and gently fold them into the batter.

4. Cook the waffles according to your waffle iron's instructions. The finished waffles can be kept warm in a 150°F oven. For crisper waffles, place on a baking sheet; for softer waffles, cover the baking sheet with foil. Serve hot.

Banana–Poppy Seed Waffles

Substitute 1 tablespoon poppy seeds for the
pecans or walnuts. Proceed as directed.

WAKE UP

Five A.M. A nun or monk walks the halls of the monastery each morning, ringing a
bell, waking the sleeping residents. The enormous bell that sits outside the main
entrance on top of a small hill is then struck every minute or so by the person leading
the morning chanting service, until he or she is signaled that the morning service is
about to begin. If we happen to fall asleep again after hearing the small bell, the reso-
nant sound of the large bell gently nudges us awake. We don our robes and straggle
into the zendo one by one. By 5:20 A.M., we are all there. The large bell continues its
sonorous rhythm.

   If you listen carefully, you will notice that the sound of one strike fades completely
before the next one begins.

—Myochi

Golden Granola

We make granola in large batches since it can be stored for several weeks, but we always finish it long before that. Occasionally, I serve granola for breakfast, but most of it is consumed for dinners or snacks. If you can't find rye and wheat flakes in your local natural food store, substitute additional rolled oats.

MAKES ABOUT 8½ CUPS

DRY INGREDIENTS

1½ cups old-fashioned rolled oats
1 cup rolled rye flakes (optional)
1 cup rolled wheat flakes (optional)
½ cup wheat germ, toasted (see page 6)
½ cup soy flour
½ cup chopped walnuts, toasted (see page 6)
⅓ cup chopped almonds, toasted (see page 6)
¼ cup sesame seeds, toasted (see page 6)
¼ cup sunflower seeds, toasted (see page 6)

WET INGREDIENTS

½ cup unsweetened applesauce
¼ cup plus 2 tablespoons honey
¼ cup plus 2 tablespoons maple syrup
¼ cup canola or corn oil
2 tablespoons vanilla extract

¾ cup dried fruit (raisins, currants, apricots, dates), chopped

1. Preheat the oven to 350°F.

2. DRY INGREDIENTS: Combine the dry ingredients thoroughly in a large bowl and make a well in the center.

3. WET INGREDIENTS: Whisk together the wet ingredients in a medium bowl. Pour into the dry ingredients and mix until evenly moistened.

4. Spread on a large baking sheet and bake, stirring every 10 minutes, until the granola begins to turn golden brown, about 30 minutes.

5. Remove from the oven and immediately pour the granola into a large bowl. Add the dried fruit and stir well. Let cool completely and store in an airtight container at room temperature.

NOTE: You can use all honey or all maple syrup instead of a combination.

" 'Today I am' is the essential condition and that is no other than the essence of Zen Buddhism."

— Eido Roshi

Sautéed Gingered Apples

Serve this versatile topping over hot cereal, waffles, pancakes, yogurt, or ice cream. The apples are also terrific on top of Oatmeal-Raisin Pudding (page 215). They can be cooked in advance and refrigerated.

MAKES ABOUT 2 CUPS

4   Gala, Rome, Fuji, McIntosh, or other firm apples, peeled, cored, and cut into ⅛-inch-thick slices
½   teaspoon ground cinnamon
5   tablespoons unsalted butter
1   2-inch piece ginger, peeled and grated (see note)
1   tablespoon maple syrup
1   teaspoon vanilla extract
¼   teaspoon ground allspice
¼   teaspoon ground fennel seeds
⅛   teaspoon freshly grated nutmeg
2   pinches freshly milled black pepper
    Pinch ground cloves

Toss the apples with the cinnamon in a large bowl. Melt the butter over medium-low heat in a large skillet. Add the apple mixture, ginger, maple syrup, and vanilla to the skillet and mix well. Stir in the remaining spices, cover, and cook, stirring occasionally, until the apples are tender, about 30 minutes. Serve warm.

TO PEEL AND GRATE GINGER: Hold the root in one hand and scrape the skin off with the edge of a spoon or a vegetable peeler. Grate the ginger on a grater or on a Microplane Zester (see page 243), or slice thinly into coin-shaped slices and chop in a food processor.

Fruit Compote

Seiko Susan Morningstar, a close friend and resident nun, taught me how to concoct this scrumptious fruit compote. She frequently makes it for informal breakfasts on rest days, and it has become a favorite of guests and residents alike. Serve the compote warm or chilled, with yogurt, Banana Pecan Waffles (page 18), or Oatmeal Pancakes (page 17).

MAKES ABOUT 3 CUPS

2 cups orange juice
1 cup dried apricots
1 cup prunes
½ cup raisins
½ cup dried cherries, pears, apples, or other dried fruit
½ cup dry red wine
1 tablespoon maple syrup, plus more if desired
2 teaspoons vanilla extract
¼ teaspoon ground cinnamon
¼ teaspoon ground allspice
⅛ teaspoon ground cardamom
2 teaspoons grated orange zest
1 teaspoon grated lemon zest

1. Combine the orange juice, dried fruits, wine, 1 tablespoon maple syrup, vanilla, cinnamon, allspice, and cardamom in a large saucepan and bring to a boil over medium-high heat. Reduce the heat to low and simmer, uncovered, stirring occasionally, until most of the liquid has been reduced, about 20 minutes.

2. Stir in the orange and lemon zests. Sweeten with more maple syrup, if desired. Serve warm or chilled.

GREAT

BROWN, WHITE, OR BASMATI RICE IS THE FOUNDATION OF MANY OF OUR formal meals. I cook it at least every other day in one form or another for lunch. Traditionally, monks who beg from door to door for their monastery in Japan collect rice more than any other bestowal, since rice fields abound, and with only the offerings to cook with, the monastery cook serves rice daily. Because of this archetype, rice has become a staple at Dai Bosatsu as well.

Especially after long periods of zazen meditation, the sight of a big, nourishing, and piping hot bowl of brown rice making its way down the table is comforting. Rice can serve as a substantial backdrop for countless other dishes, for it has the ability to unify many different flavors in traditional dishes of many cultures.

Basmati Rice with Raisins and Walnuts is a wonderful complement to curry from many countries, including Japanese-Style Curry and Almond Thai Curry. Shiitake Rice will balance any Asian-style meal, whether as a small side dish or a substantial accompaniment to a dish like Tofu Sashimi Platter.

Although most of the recipes in this chapter are simple, they are not plain. The addition of one or two vegetables and some familiar seasonings can transform plain rice into a savory treat. Other recipes in this chapter, such as Spicy Rice Bake with Black-Eyed Peas, Collard Greens, and Sweet Potato, are more complex. These dishes require a little more preparation and are reserved for days when I have more time.

—Seppo

Brown Rice with Quinoa

The addition of quinoa to brown rice gives a nutritional boost and a lighter result. This dish is a good choice if you want something a bit more delicate than brown rice alone.

MAKES 4 TO 6 SERVINGS

1½ cups short-grain brown rice, rinsed well and drained
1 cup quinoa, rinsed well and drained
Tamari

1. Bring 3 cups water to a boil in a medium saucepan. Add the rice, return to a boil, reduce the heat to very low, cover, and cook, without removing the lid, until tender, about 50 minutes. Let stand covered for 10 minutes.

2. Meanwhile, bring 2 cups water to a boil in a separate medium saucepan. Add the quinoa and return to a boil. Reduce the heat to very low, cover, and cook, without removing the lid, until tender, about 20 minutes. Remove from the heat and let stand covered until the rice is done.

3. Fluff the quinoa and mix it gently but thoroughly into the rice, using the side of a wooden spoon so as not to break up the grains of rice. Serve hot with tamari on the side.

Shiitake Rice

The shiitake mushrooms lend their meaty essence to this luscious rice, and a splash of tamari draws forth its full flavor. Serve with a mild-flavored dish, such as Tofu Sashimi Platter (page 72) or Quick Miso Soup (page 135).

MAKES 6 TO 8 SERVINGS

8 dried shiitake mushrooms
2 teaspoons tamari
½ teaspoon sea salt
2 cups short-grain brown rice, rinsed well and drained

1. Bring 4 cups water and the mushrooms to a boil in a medium saucepan. Reduce the heat to low, cover, and simmer for 1 hour. Transfer the mushrooms to a medium bowl with a slotted spoon. Strain the broth through a fine sieve or a coffee filter placed in a strainer set over a medium bowl to remove any dirt. Set the broth aside.

2. Thoroughly clean the mushrooms in cold water, running your fingers under the gills to remove any silt. Blot the mushrooms dry, cut off and discard the stems, and thinly slice the caps.

3. Add enough water to the mushroom broth to measure 4¼ cups. Place in a large saucepan, add the tamari and salt, and bring to a boil. Add the rice and sliced mushrooms and return to a boil. Reduce the heat to very low, cover, and cook, without removing the lid, until the rice is tender, about 50 minutes. Let stand covered for 10 minutes, then fluff and serve.

Spinach Rice

A little tamari and mirin mixed with the spinach gives this rice a rich flavor. I make it when I am pressed for time but want to serve something slightly more elaborate than plain rice.

MAKES 6 TO 8 SERVINGS

2 tablespoons tamari
1 tablespoon mirin
1 teaspoon olive oil
2 cups short-grain brown rice, rinsed well and drained
½ teaspoon sea salt
1 10-ounce package frozen (not thawed) chopped spinach

1. Bring the tamari, mirin, olive oil, and enough water to equal 4 cups to a boil in a large saucepan. Add the rice and salt, return to a boil, reduce the heat to very low, cover, and simmer, without removing the lid, until tender, about 50 minutes. Let stand covered for 10 minutes.

2. Bring ½ cup water to a boil in a medium saucepan. Add the spinach, breaking it up, reduce the heat to medium, cover, and simmer for about 5 minutes. Drain well.

3. Mix the spinach gently but thoroughly into the rice, using the side of a wooden spoon so as not to break up the grains of rice, and serve immediately.

PAY ATTENTION

Once we reach Beecher Lake, which sits on top of the last stretch of road to the monastery, after a narrow two-mile climb forty-five minutes away from the main highway, I find myself letting out such a long, deep breath that you might think I'd been holding it the whole way up. This sigh springs from the pleasure of coming home.

The lake materializes in front of us when we come over the last tiny crest. If we aren't careful and mindful that the road curves sharply to the left at the edge of the lake, it would be easy to drive straight into it. It's as if the lake were a Zen welcoming mat, greeting us, and exhorting us to PAY ATTENTION! Our first Rinzai Zen lesson.

—Myochi

Rice with Carrot and Hijiki

The classic Japanese combination of hijiki and carrot makes a delightful addition to rice. The carrot imparts a subtle sweetness, while the hijiki lends a slight nutty flavor. This dish can be served as a main dish or a side dish.

MAKES 6 TO 8 SERVINGS

2 tablespoons tamari
2 cups short-grain brown rice, rinsed well and drained
1 large carrot, grated
1 teaspoon sea salt
1 cup apple juice
½ ounce dried hijiki

1. Bring the tamari and enough water to equal 4 cups to a boil in a large saucepan. Add the rice, carrot, and salt and return to a boil. Reduce the heat to very low, cover, and simmer, without removing the lid, until the rice is tender, about 50 minutes. Let stand covered for 10 minutes so the starches in the rice firm up.

2. Meanwhile, bring the apple juice to a boil in a small saucepan. Remove from the heat, add the hijiki, cover, and let stand for 30 minutes. Drain the hijiki; discard the apple juice.

3. Mix the hijiki gently but thoroughly into the rice, using the side of a wooden spoon, so as not to break up the grains of rice. Serve immediately.

Ginger-Burdock Rice

The naturally sweet flavor and crisp texture of burdock blends with the gentle bite of ginger to provide a well-rounded flavor. Serve with Tofu Sashimi Platter (page 72), Asian-Style Tortilla Rolls (page 74), or Sautéed Tofu with Spinach and Hijiki (page 68).

MAKES 6 TO 8 SERVINGS

½ burdock root, peeled (see below)
2 tablespoons tamari, plus more for serving
2 cups short-grain brown rice, rinsed well and drained
1 1-inch piece ginger, peeled and grated

1. Thinly slice the burdock diagonally, then slice each piece lengthwise to make 4 to 8 toothpick-size strips. Soak the burdock in water for 30 minutes. Rinse and drain.

2. Bring 4¼ cups water and the tamari to a boil in a large saucepan. Add the rice, burdock, and ginger, return to a boil, reduce the heat to very low, cover, and cook, without removing the lid, until the rice is tender, about 50 minutes. Let stand covered for 10 minutes, then fluff and serve with extra tamari on the side.

TO PREPARE BURDOCK: Although American texts instruct you not to peel burdock because the highest concentration of nutrients lies directly beneath the skin, I always do so. If you are not going to peel the burdock, submerge the roots in water and wash them well with a brush.

Don't use a vegetable peeler, because it will remove too much flesh. Instead, use the back of a paring knife. Hold the dull side of the blade firmly against the root and scrape away from you. You can also use the edge of a spoon. Or use a piece of tightly crumpled aluminum foil that you have recycled. Briskly rub the foil back and forth down the length of the root. As you peel, rinse the root and the peeling utensil occasionally. Burdock tends to oxidize and turn brown quickly after peeling, whether soaked in water or not. After slicing, soak the burdock in water for 20 to 30 minutes. This discoloration does not affect taste.

Basmati Rice with Raisins and Walnuts

The sweet raisins and toasted walnuts harmonize well with the flavor of basmati rice. I serve this rice with Almond Thai Curry (page 64) or Japanese-Style Curry (page 66).

MAKES 6 TO 8 SERVINGS

½ cup raisins
4 cups Basic Vegetable Stock (page 134) or water
2 cups white or brown basmati rice, rinsed well and drained
2 pinches turmeric (optional)
¾ cup chopped walnuts, toasted (see page 6)

1. Bring 1 cup water to a boil in a small saucepan. Remove from the heat, add the raisins, cover, and let stand for 30 minutes. Drain and set aside.

2. Bring the stock or water to a boil in a large saucepan. Add the rice and turmeric, if using, and return to a boil. Reduce the heat to very low, cover, and simmer, without removing the lid, until tender, about 30 minutes.

3. Mix the raisins and walnuts gently but thoroughly into the rice, using the side of a wooden spoon so as not to break up the grains of rice, and serve.

MORNING MEETING

Every day immediately after breakfast, the residents of the monastery congregate for a morning meeting, still dressed in their meditation robes. This is at once a formal and an informal occasion. It begins formally with chanting and a reading for the day. Coffee and tea are then served, and casual conversation and discussion ensues for ten to twenty minutes. Following this, the day's work assignments are given out. The jisha, who acts as the caretaking monk, introduces and welcomes guests who arrived the previous evening or bids farewell to those departing that day. The maintenance manager updates the community on any ongoing projects. Residents tell stories that relate to the monastery. There is often much laughter. Yet even in the somewhat relaxed atmosphere of this meeting, an underlying tone of seriousness and a certain decorum are maintained, especially when the abbot, Eido Roshi, is in attendance.

At one meeting, Roshi spent some time correcting the way some of the instruments had been struck that morning. The substitute tenzo had hit the meal gong too quickly — there was to be more of a pause between strikes. Another monk's rhythm was also too quick. And the jikijitsu, the head monk of the zendo, was too slow — he needed to pick it up. In each case, Roshi demonstrated the proper rhythm. Everyone paid attention, for even though he was addressing the three musicians, there was a broader message to all of us: "Take care in all that you do, pay attention, and don't be lazy; even the simple task of striking a bell is important."

Though it's not required that we sit in zazen posture in these meetings, most of us do so. One morning years ago, Roshi admonished a new student who was leaning up against the wall and sent a clear message to the rest of us: "If you don't develop your own spine, you'll have to carry that wall around with you wherever you go."

—Myochi

Dirty Rice

This southern favorite is usually made with browned bits of meat. Browned onion, tempeh, shiitake mushrooms, and tamari give this vegetarian version its traditional meaty flavor.

MAKES 4 TO 6 SERVINGS

6 dried shiitake mushrooms
1½ teaspoons sesame oil
1½ teaspoons canola or corn oil
½ medium onion, minced
1 teaspoon sea salt
4 ounces tempeh, crumbled or cut into tiny pieces
1 large celery rib, diced
3 garlic cloves, minced
1 tablespoon plus 2 teaspoons tamari
  About 1 cup Basic Vegetable Stock (page 134) or water
2 cups short-grain brown rice, rinsed well and drained

1. Bring 4 cups cold water and the mushrooms to a boil in a medium saucepan. Reduce the heat to low, cover, and simmer for 1 hour. Transfer the mushrooms to a medium bowl with a slotted spoon. Strain the broth through a fine sieve or a coffee filter placed in a strainer set over a medium bowl to remove any dirt. Set the broth aside.

2. Thoroughly clean the mushrooms in cold water, running your fingers under the gills to remove any silt. Blot the mushrooms dry, cut off and discard the stems, and mince the caps.

3. Heat both oils in a large skillet over medium-high heat. Add the onion and salt and sauté, stirring occasionally, until the onion begins to soften, about 2 minutes.

4. Add the tempeh, celery, mushrooms, garlic, and tamari. Continue to sauté over medium-high heat, stirring occasionally and scraping the bottom, until the tempeh mixture begin to stick to the skillet, about 10 minutes. Scrape up as much as you can from the bottom of the skillet.

5. Add enough stock or water to the mushroom broth to measure 4 cups. Place the broth, tempeh mixture, and rice in a large saucepan and bring to a boil. Reduce the heat to very low, cover, and simmer, without removing the lid, until the rice is tender, about 50 minutes. Let stand covered for 10 minutes so the starches firm up. Stir to distribute the ingredients and fluff the rice with the side of a wooden spoon. Serve.

"A monk asked the Chinese Zen master Ummon, 'What is moment after moment's Samadhi?'

Ummon replied, 'Rice in the bowl, water in the pail.'"

— From *The Blue Rock Collection*, translated by Eido Roshi

Spicy Rice Bake with Black-Eyed Peas, Collard Greens, and Sweet Potato

This one-dish meal has a southern flair and the rich consistency of a jambalaya. Serve with Ginger-Butternut Biscuits (page 180).

MAKES 4 TO 6 SERVINGS

2 tablespoons olive oil
1 medium onion, diced
½ teaspoon sea salt
6–8 garlic cloves, minced
1 medium sweet potato, peeled and cut into ½-inch dice (2½–3 cups)
6 large collard green leaves, large ribs removed, leaves torn in half lengthwise and cut into ½-inch strips
1½ cups short-grain brown rice, rinsed well and drained
1 cup black-eyed peas, sorted, rinsed well, and drained
1 tablespoon Chipotle Paste (page 192) or ½ teaspoon cayenne pepper
¼ cup tamari
1 tablespoon balsamic vinegar

1. Preheat the oven to 350°F.

2. Heat the oil in a large skillet over medium-high heat. Add the onion and salt and sauté, stirring occasionally, until the onion begins to soften, about 2 minutes. Add the garlic and sauté until the onion is almost translucent, 3 to 4 minutes more. Stir in the sweet potato and collard greens and sauté, stirring occasionally, until the collard greens are bright green (don't let them turn dark green) and wilted, about 5 minutes.

3. Place the rice and black-eyed peas in a 9-x-13-inch baking dish. Add the sweet potato mixture and the chipotle paste or cayenne and mix well. Pour 6 cups boiling water, the tamari, and balsamic vinegar into the baking dish and mix carefully. Cover tightly with foil and bake for 1½ hours, or until the rice and black-eyed peas are tender. Stir gently and serve hot.

WASHING FLOORS

An air of casual elegance with an underlying sense of formality and tradition pervades the monastery. Everything is clean, neat, and uncluttered. A place for everything and everything in its place. There's plenty of work to go around for the twelve to thirty full-time residents.

The monastery method of washing floors is both efficient and unusual. First, you put some Murphy's Oil Soap in a large bucket of water. Only a small amount is needed, because shoes are never worn inside and the floors don't get very dirty. Using too much soap would make the floors too slick and hence dangerous. Everything is well thought out — even this simple chore.

You wring out the rag so that it's damp, not dripping wet. Then you place the rag on the floor under the heels of both hands, about shoulder width apart. You rise up on the balls of your feet (no socks!), making an inverted V with your body, so that your bottom is up in the air. You bend your knees, pushing the rag along the floor in front of you, and walk forward briskly. It's awkward at first, and if the rag is too wet, it won't glide smoothly, but after a few tries, you find yourself racing along, getting a bit of a workout and cleaning the floors to boot. It's impossible to be lazy about it, in mind or body. The task is difficult and refreshing at the same time. It makes you question what is essential, even for a chore as simple as washing the floor.

—Myochi

Mushroom and Sun-Dried Tomato Risotto

Risotto is a traditional Italian specialty made with Arborio rice (see page 235). The finished dish is delectable and creamy, with the rice grains remaining firm and separate. This risotto was inspired by one made with the help of my friend Martin Cowart, chef and Manhattan restaurateur, on a day when we found ourselves without much fresh produce.

MAKES 4 TO 6 SERVINGS

1½ ounces sun-dried tomatoes (½–¾ cup)
 8 tablespoons olive oil or 4 tablespoons olive oil and
      4 tablespoons (½ stick) unsalted butter
10–12 ounces white mushrooms, cut into
      ¼-inch-thick slices
4¼ cups Basic Vegetable Stock (page 134) or water
 ½ medium onion, minced
 ½ teaspoon sea salt, plus more to taste
 2 garlic cloves, minced
1½ cups Arborio rice
 ½ cup dry red wine
 ½ cup ricotta cheese
 ½ cup freshly grated Parmesan or Asiago cheese,
      plus more for serving
   Freshly milled black pepper
 1 tablespoon chopped fresh rosemary or basil (optional)

1. Bring 1 cup water to a boil in a small saucepan. Remove from the heat, add the sun-dried tomatoes, and cover. Let stand, stirring occasionally, until tender, about 45 minutes. Drain the tomatoes, reserving the soaking liquid, cool, and slice thinly. Set aside.

2. Heat 2 tablespoons of the oil (or 1 tablespoon oil and 1 tablespoon butter) in a large skillet over high heat. Add the mushrooms and sauté, stirring frequently, just until they begin to soften and exude their juices, about 3 minutes. Immediately transfer the mushrooms and their juices to a medium bowl and set aside.

3. Bring the stock or water and the tomato-soaking liquid to a boil in a medium saucepan. Cover and keep warm over low heat.

4. Heat the remaining 6 tablespoons oil (or the remaining 3 tablespoons oil and 3 tablespoons butter) in a large saucepan over medium-high heat. Add the onion and salt and sauté, stirring occasionally, until the onion begins to soften, about 2 minutes. Add the sun-dried tomatoes and garlic and sauté until the onion is translucent, 3 to 4 minutes more.

5. Add the rice to the onion mixture and sauté, stirring constantly, for 2 minutes. Reduce the heat to medium-low, add ½ cup of the hot stock or water and cook, stirring frequently until absorbed.

Continue, adding ½ cup of stock or water at a time, stirring frequently and waiting for it to be absorbed before adding the next measure. This should take 20 to 25 minutes.

6. Add the wine to the risotto and stir until it is completely absorbed. Add the ricotta, Parmesan or Asiago, and mushrooms and continue to cook, stirring, until the cheese is incorporated and all the liquid is absorbed, about 5 minutes. Season with salt and pepper to taste. Serve topped with the rosemary or basil, if using, and pass additional grated Parmesan or Asiago at the table.

JUST EATING

Each of the formal meals at the monastery is conducted in a mere half hour. The time spent chanting before and after, serving the food, and cleaning up leaves little opportunity to eat.

No time to dawdle, no need to talk. Mealtime is about "just eating." But in the same way that "just sitting" involves more, such as correct posture, breathing, and concentration, "just eating" is about more than just eating. It is about gratitude, mindfulness, and bringing one's awareness to the big picture—where the food comes from, why we're all here, and what our common purpose is.

— Myochi

Stir-Fried Basmati Rice

This dish is a fulfilling and colorful medley of rice, crisp-tender vegetables, and tofu mildly seasoned with Mediterranean spices. Serve with Quick Miso Soup (page 135) and a tossed green salad.

MAKES 4 TO 6 SERVINGS

1 cup white or brown basmati rice, rinsed well and drained
2 tablespoons sesame oil
1 medium onion, chopped
½ teaspoon sea salt
1 1½-inch piece ginger, peeled and grated
2 garlic cloves, minced
½ pound green beans, trimmed and cut into ⅛-inch pieces
1 red bell pepper, ribbed, seeded, and diced
2 large celery ribs, chopped
4 ounces firm tofu, diced
2 large carrots, grated
¾ teaspoon ground coriander
½ teaspoon ground cumin
½ cup chopped walnuts, toasted (see page 6)
1 tablespoon tamari
  Freshly milled black pepper

1. Bring 1½ cups water to a boil in a small saucepan. Add the rice, reduce the heat to very low and cover. Cook, without removing the lid, until tender, about 25 minutes. Remove from the heat, fluff with a fork, and set aside.

2. Heat the oil in a large skillet over medium-high heat. Add the onion and salt and sauté, stirring occasionally, until the onion begins to soften, about 2 minutes. Add the ginger and garlic and sauté until the onion is translucent, about 5 minutes more. Add the green beans, bell pepper, celery, and tofu and sauté, stirring occasionally, until the vegetables begin to soften, 5 to 8 minutes. Stir in the carrots, coriander, and cumin and sauté until the vegetables are cooked to the desired tenderness, 2 to 5 minutes more.

3. Add the rice and walnuts to the skillet. Toss to mix and heat through. Add the tamari and pepper to taste and serve.

NOODLES

WIND

Soba with Shiitake Dashi 44

Udon with Kombu Dashi 48

Szechuan Green Beans and Soba 50

Penne with Broccoli Rabe 52

Orzo with Tempeh and Eggplant 54

Spaghetti with Chipotle and
    Garlic 55

Pasta Puttanesca 58

Classic Marinara Sauce 60

ONCE A MONTH, THE GATES OF THE MONASTERY ARE CLOSED TO ORDINARY visitors for a week of concentrated meditation called *sesshin*, which means "to collect the mind." Our days begin at 4:30 A.M. and are filled with zazen meditation, lectures by Eido Roshi, individual interviews with him, a short work period, and three meals. The fourth day of sesshin is known as the "middle day," and it is also referred to as "noodle day."

Whereas brown rice is served every other day during sesshin, udon or soba noodles are offered on the middle day to celebrate the halfway mark. It's a welcome change — a reward and a gratifying bowl of comfort and encouragement.

The many condiments, such as thinly sliced scallions, bits of nori, freshly grated ginger and daikon, and ground sesame seeds, are served in separate bowls. Diners help themselves, adding as much or as little as they prefer to their broth. Noodles are traditionally consumed with chopsticks by lowering them into the separate bowls of broth until they are almost entirely submerged, raising the bowl to the mouth, and then slurping the noodles quickly with a cooling intake of breath and a sucking sound, which cools the hot noodles and blends the exquisite flavors.

— Seppo

Soba with Shiitake Dashi

Soba are thin, delicate noodles made from buckwheat. I serve soba with dashi, a light broth traditionally made from sea vegetables, fish, or shiitake mushrooms. All of the components can be prepared in advance: the soba is served at room temperature, and the dashi simply needs to be reheated.

MAKES 4 TO 6 SERVINGS

SHIITAKE DASHI
 8   dried shiitake mushrooms
 ¾   cup sake
 ½   cup tamari
 1   tablespoon mirin
 2   pinches sea salt
 ¼   teaspoon fresh lemon juice

2½ pounds soba noodles

CONDIMENTS
 2   sheets nori (see opposite page), thinly shredded
 4   scallions, thinly sliced on the diagonal (see opposite page)
 2   tablespoons sesame seeds, toasted (see page 6) and ground
 2   teaspoons wasabi powder (see opposite page), mixed with just enough water to form a soft paste
 1   2-inch piece daikon, peeled and grated
 1   2-inch piece ginger, peeled and grated

1. DASHI: Bring 2¾ cups water and the mushrooms to a boil in a small saucepan. Reduce the heat to low, cover, and simmer for 1 hour. Transfer the mushrooms to a small bowl with a slotted spoon and reserve for another use. Strain the broth through a fine sieve or a coffee filter placed in a strainer set over a medium saucepan to remove any dirt.

2. Add the sake, tamari, mirin, and salt to the mushroom broth and bring to a boil. Reduce the heat to low and simmer until the alcohol aroma disappears, about 15 minutes. Remove from the heat, add the lemon juice, and serve immediately or cover and set aside. If the dashi is too strong for your taste, dilute it with hot water.

3. Meanwhile, bring a large pot of water to a boil and cook the soba to the desired doneness, 5 to 8 minutes. Drain, rinse well under cold water, using your hands to gently swish the noodles, and drain again. Repeat. Serve immediately or place in a colander, cover with a damp cloth, and set aside.

4. CONDIMENTS: Divide the soba among 4 to 6 serving bowls, swirling each serving into a mound, and sprinkle with the nori. Place ½ to ¾ cup hot dashi in separate individual bowls alongside each serving of soba. Serve the remaining condiments on a small platter or in little bowls at the center of the table so the diners can help themselves.

TO SHRED NORI: Several sheets of nori can be cut at once. With the short side toward you, cut with scissors or a very sharp knife along the length of the long side, making 4 equal strips, about 2 inches wide. Stack the strips and cut through them as thinly as possible to form dainty toothpick-size strips.

TO CUT SCALLIONS ON THE DIAGONAL: This is a traditional Japanese cut. Slice only 1 scallion at a time. Slice the scallion every ⅛ to ¼ inch on a very sharp diagonal (at least 45°). Keep the tip of your knife on the cutting board and pull it toward you, sliding it on the board and slicing through the scallion. This will give you a much cleaner cut than chopping down through the scallion.

TO MAKE WASABI PASTE: Mix the wasabi powder with just enough cold water to form a soft paste. Let stand covered for 10 minutes. The flavor will develop, and the paste will firm up a bit. Prepare as close to serving time as possible and make only as much as you need; its strong punch doesn't last long. Commercial packaged wasabi paste can be used directly from the tube or jar.

TO PREPARE IN ADVANCE: The dashi can be made a few days in advance, stored in the refrigerator, and reheated just before serving. The soba noodles can be cooked a few hours ahead. Rinse and drain the noodles every 45 minutes or so — whenever they start sticking together. The sesame and nori can be prepared a few days before serving and stored at room temperature in an airtight container. The remaining condiments should be prepared the day of serving and refrigerated. Grate the ginger and make the wasabi paste no more than 1 hour before serving.

SESSHIN

Sesshin is an intense, silent, seven-day period of zazen, or meditation. Anywhere from thirty to eighty Zen students, monks, and nuns come from all over the world to participate. Sesshin is the crux of all Zen practice. During this period, we rise earlier than usual, at 4:30 A.M., and retire later, at 10:00 P.M. There is one hour of work practice a day and a short break after meals. Sometimes a yoga class is offered twice a day for those who want it. Other than this, we sit in the zendo in zazen posture, we chant, we sit, we sit, and we sit some more. Oddly enough, as the week goes on, it gets easier. Our bodies adjust to the rigor; they give in, give up, and relax into themselves. We stop fighting, stop trying to control, and let ourselves be guided by our higher selves — a lesson that serves us well when we return to our real lives.

Sesshins are usually scheduled to commemorate certain holidays — Buddha's birthday, Buddha's enlightenment day, the monastery's anniversary, for example — and often take place during the full-moon week, which adds to the intensity. The names of the sesshins — Holy Days, Memorial Day, Anniversary, Golden Wind, and Harvest — give a clue to the time of year. During sesshin, we sit for at least twelve hours a day. Many people choose to sit even longer, returning to the zendo after 10:00 P.M. to work on their koans or to push through their own resistance. At rohatsu sesshin, which is the last one of the year and commemorates Buddha's enlightenment, everyone sits more. One full day is added to the usual schedule, and, starting on the third day, extra sitting time is added to the end of the day, so that by the last day, we all sit until midnight. Nearly one hundred hours of sitting still during this week! Pain cannot be avoided. Pain in the legs, joints, knees. Sometimes the hands and feet swell. The back aches. We get little sleep. Time stretches, and a week seems longer than seven days. Breathing, counting one's breath, working on a koan, concentrating to get beyond the pain. Why am I here? What am I doing?

Every afternoon we are treated to a formal talk by Eido Roshi. These usually inspire and encourage us to push on, especially during the first few days when many of us feel like giving up. As Roshi likes to say, sesshin, like most things in life, takes perseverance, endurance, and patience. Once we accept the pain, it no longer exists or at least no longer tortures us. Sometimes sitting is easier and more rewarding if there is pain. Pain keeps us awake, alert, and in the moment.

Even though there is a strict rule of silence, there is support for one another. The silence purifies our communication. At some point, understanding and relief come. Sesshin becomes a seamless stream of awareness, with each activity blending into the whole: sitting, bowing, chanting. And when we sit down to eat, our taste buds are piqued and radiant with sesshin mind.

—Myochi

Udon with Kombu Dashi

Long, thick udon noodles are traditionally served swimming in a large bowl of boiling water. Because the water from the serving bowl clings to the noodles, the strength of the dashi is diluted when the udon noodles are dunked into it. Thus, this dashi is heartier than the shiitake dashi I serve with soba noodles (see page 44).

MAKES 4 TO 6 SERVINGS

KOMBU DASHI

- 1 4-x-5-inch piece kombu
- 1 cup sake
- ¼ cup plus 3 tablespoons tamari
- 2 teaspoons mirin
- ¼ teaspoon fresh lemon juice

2½ pounds udon noodles

CONDIMENTS

- 2 sheets nori (see page 45), thinly shredded
- 4 scallions, thinly sliced on the diagonal (see opposite page)
- 2 tablespoons sesame seeds, toasted (see page 6) and ground
- 1 2-inch piece daikon, peeled and grated
- 1 2-inch piece ginger, peeled and grated

1. DASHI: Wipe the kombu with a wet cloth. Place the kombu in a large saucepan with 3 cups cold water and let stand at room temperature for 1 hour. Place the saucepan over medium-high heat until the water just begins to boil. Immediately remove and discard the kombu and strain the broth through a fine sieve or a coffee filter in a strainer set over a medium saucepan to remove any dirt.

2. Add the sake, tamari, and mirin to the kombu broth and bring to a boil. Reduce the heat to low and simmer until the alcohol aroma disappears, about 15 minutes. Remove from the heat, add the lemon juice, and serve immediately or cover and set aside. If the dashi is too strong for your taste, dilute it with hot water.

3. Meanwhile, bring a medium pot of water and a large pot of water to a boil. Cook the udon in the large pot until al dente (it will absorb more water later in the serving bowl), about 10 minutes. Drain. Place the udon in a large serving bowl and cover with the boiling water from the medium pot.

4. Place ½ to ¾ cup hot dashi in each of 4 individual bowls. Serve the condiments on a small platter or in little bowls in the center of the table so the diners can help themselves.

TO PREPARE IN ADVANCE: The dashi can be made a few days ahead, stored in the refrigerator, and reheated just before serving. The udon noodles can be cooked up to 1 hour ahead. When the noodles are ready, refresh them with cold water and drain. Before you place them in the serving bowl with boiling water, submerge them in hot tap water baths and swish them around a bit. This will warm them and prevent them from sticking. The sesame and nori can be prepared a few days before serving and stored at room temperature in airtight containers. The remaining condiments should be prepared the day of serving and refrigerated. Grate the ginger and make the wasabi paste no more than 1 hour before serving.

"To understand Zen practice, we must first of all realize that body, breath, and mind are to be regarded as one inseparable unit."

— Eido Roshi

Szechuan Green Beans and Soba

This unique and delicious soba dish is adapted from a recipe by Bettina Vitell, a dear friend, dharma sister, and past tenzo at Dai Bosatsu, which was published in her first cookbook, *A Taste of Heaven and Earth*. You can vary the spiciness by adding more or less red pepper flakes. Serve with Cucumber-Grape Raita with Tofu (page 120) or a green salad tossed with Red Grape Dressing (page 131) or Strawberry-Cilantro Dressing (page 130).

MAKES 2 TO 4 SERVINGS

12 ounces soba noodles
1 tablespoon plus 1 teaspoon sesame oil
2 teaspoons canola or corn oil
1 pound green beans, trimmed and cut into
    bite-size pieces
4 garlic cloves, minced
½ teaspoon red pepper flakes
3–4 tablespoons tamari, plus more for serving
2 tablespoons sesame seeds, toasted (see page 6; optional)

1. Bring a large pot of water to a boil and cook the soba until al dente, about 5 minutes. Drain, rinse under cold water, and drain again. Place the noodles in a large bowl and set aside.

2. Heat both oils in a large skillet over medium-high heat. Add the green beans and sauté, stirring occasionally, for 3 minutes. Reduce the heat to low and cook, stirring occasionally, for 2 minutes more. Add the garlic and red pepper flakes and cook, stirring constantly, for 2 minutes more. Immediately pour the green bean mixture over the soba noodles, scraping the skillet well to get all the oil into the bowl.

3. Toss the soba and the green bean mixture until the beans are evenly distributed and the soba is coated with oil. Add the tamari and toss again. Place in a serving bowl and garnish with the sesame seeds, if using. Serve with extra tamari on the side.

NOTES: It's very important not to cook the green beans over high heat. Sesame oil has a very low smoking point, and high heat will burn it.

    This dish can be made several hours in advance and served at room temperature, but do not add the tamari until just before serving.

MIDDLE DAY

It's uncanny how much can be communicated without words or eye contact. During sesshin, no watches are worn and no talking is allowed. We are instructed to pay attention, concentrate on our own practice, and not look around. While this practice may sound severe, it is also amazingly liberating. There is no need for talk. We are each in our own small world but very definitely a part of a larger one. It would be nearly impossible to get through such a week alone, so we support and encourage each other in the silence. After a while, the mood of the group becomes our mood and vice versa.

By the middle day, it is as though we are one body, one mind. Without even looking, we know that everyone wears a hidden smile — we are halfway through and sure that we'll make it to the end! It is an electric feeling that begins as soon as the day opens. The activities marking the midpoint of the week contribute to the celebratory air. The afternoon tea ceremony is one of the daily events that is celebrated in a special way. Powdered green tea and a small sweet are served. Six monks, three for each side of the zendo, serve the tea to the rest of us. The first measures the powdered tea into each cup, the second pours the water, and the third whisks it to a frothy broth. The taste of this pungent tea, along with the sweet, is a delectable treat, our reward for making it to the middle day.

One time the middle day fell on Halloween. The tenzos surprised us all when we walked into supper. Greeted with carved pumpkins on the dining room altar, their countenances lit up by the candles inside, we couldn't help but smile ourselves. A treat for each of us had been hidden in our bowls — a piece of Halloween candy. We stole glances at one another and basked for a moment in the contagious atmosphere of delight. By the middle day, even little things are momentous.

—Myochi

Penne with Broccoli Rabe

Sweet toasted wheat germ, bitter broccoli rabe, pungent Dijon mustard, and garlic—both raw and lightly sautéed—flavor this exceptional pasta dish, which is fabulous either hot or at room temperature. It's a great alternative to the traditional pasta salad for summer picnics.

MAKES 4 TO 6 SERVINGS

½ cup olive oil
10 garlic cloves, minced
3 tablespoons Dijon mustard
1 tablespoon balsamic vinegar
1 tablespoon fresh lemon juice
1 pound broccoli rabe, 1 inch trimmed off the base of the stalks, cut into 1½-inch pieces
1 tablespoon sea salt
1 pound penne (or other pasta)
¾ cup wheat germ, toasted (see page 6)
1 teaspoon red pepper flakes
Freshly grated Parmesan or Asiago cheese

1. Whisk together ¼ cup plus 2 tablespoons of the olive oil, the garlic, mustard, and vinegar in a small bowl. Measure out ¼ cup of the mixture into a large skillet. Whisk in the remaining 2 tablespoons olive oil. If you plan to serve the dish immediately, whisk the lemon juice into the oil mixture in the small bowl. If you plan to serve the dish at room temperature or chilled, reserve 2 tablespoons of the oil mixture in the small bowl; whisk in the lemon juice and toss with the pasta just before serving.

2. Bring 1½ gallons water to a boil in a large pot for the broccoli rabe and the penne. Add the broccoli rabe and salt and boil until tender, 1 to 2 minutes. Scoop the broccoli rabe from the pot with a strainer and drain.

3. Heat the oil mixture in the large skillet over medium heat, stirring occasionally, until the garlic begins to soften, 3 to 4 minutes. Stir in the broccoli rabe and keep warm over low heat, stirring occasionally.

4. Add the penne to the pot of boiling water and cook to the desired doneness, 9 to 11 minutes. Drain and place in a large serving bowl. Add the broccoli rabe mixture, scraping all the sauce from the skillet, and add the reserved oil mixture and toss well. Add the wheat germ and red pepper flakes and toss until well incorporated. Season to taste. Serve with the cheese.

NOTE: Don't combine the lemon juice with the broccoli rabe until just before serving because it will quickly discolor the florets.

"At every midday mealtime, Kingyu Osho would bring the pail of cooked rice to the front of the zendo. Dancing and laughing loudly, he would say, 'Dear Bodhisattvas, come and take your meal!'"

— From *The Blue Rock Collection,* translated by Eido Roshi

Orzo with Tempeh and Eggplant

New residents of the monastery are never quite sure what is in this dish, but they always love it. Miso lends a complex, cheeselike taste. Serve with a vegetable side dish, such as Asparagus with Lime and Tamari (page 92) or Roasted Butternut Squash (page 104), or a tossed salad.

MAKES 6 TO 8 SERVINGS

8 ounces tempeh, halved crosswise
6 tablespoons olive oil
½ medium onion, diced
¼ teaspoon sea salt
4 garlic cloves, minced
1 2-inch piece ginger, peeled and grated
1 small eggplant (about ½ pound), peeled and cut into
    ¼-inch cubes
¼ cup plus 1 teaspoon tamari
8 ounces orzo (about 1½ cups)
3 tablespoons red miso

1. Bring 4 cups water to a boil in a medium saucepan. Add the tempeh, reduce the heat to low, and simmer for 20 minutes. Drain well and let cool. Cut into ¼-inch cubes and set aside.

2. Heat ¼ cup of the oil in a large skillet over medium-high heat. Add the onion and salt and sauté, stirring occasionally, until the onion begins to soften, about 2 minutes. Add the garlic and ginger and cook, stirring constantly, for 2 minutes more. Add the tempeh, eggplant, and 3 tablespoons of the tamari and cook, stirring occasionally, until the eggplant softens, 10 to 15 minutes. Remove from the heat and set aside.

3. Heat the remaining 2 tablespoons oil and the remaining 1 tablespoon plus 1 teaspoon tamari in a large saucepan over medium heat. Add the orzo and sauté until it has absorbed the liquid and begins to stick, about 2 minutes. Add 3 cups boiling water and the miso. Whisk thoroughly until the miso dissolves. Reduce the heat to very low and cook just below a boil, stirring almost constantly, until tender and creamy, 15 to 20 minutes. Stir in more boiling water if the orzo seems too dry. Stir in the eggplant mixture and serve.

Spaghetti with Chipotle and Garlic

Fresh, ripe tomatoes combined with garlic and fiery chipotle paste produce a striking and memorable pasta sauce. Once the tomatoes and garlic are chopped, the sauce cooks right alongside the pasta and is ready at the same time, in about ten minutes. Serve with a salad and bread for a fulfilling meal.

MAKES 4 TO 6 SERVINGS

1 pound spaghetti
  Sea salt
¼ cup olive oil
4 medium tomatoes, seeded and coarsely chopped
10 garlic cloves, minced
1–2 tablespoons Chipotle Paste (page 192)
  Freshly grated Parmesan or Asiago cheese (optional)

1. Bring a large pot of salted water to a boil. Add the spaghetti and cook, stirring occasionally, until al dente, about 9 minutes. Drain well.

2. Meanwhile, heat the olive oil in a large skillet over medium-high heat. Add the tomatoes and 1 teaspoon salt and sauté, stirring occasionally, until the tomatoes begin to disintegrate, 4 to 5 minutes. Add the garlic and chipotle paste and sauté, stirring occasionally, for 4 to 5 minutes more. Taste and correct the seasonings. Toss the sauce with the pasta and serve with the cheese, if desired.

The jikijitsu is the stern but loving father of the meditation hall. *Jikijitsu* means "straight, all day," meaning one who is "present" in zazen all day and all night in order to sustain the intensity of the zendo. He sets the mood and establishes his strict rule from the minute he sits down. The zendo is his palace; he is the king, and we are his subjects. Even though we are all volunteers and choose to be sitting there, the jikijitsu's ultimate authority can sometimes rub us the wrong way. His rule may seem harsh, rigid, and severe—and to the uninitiated it does appear that way—but in the zendo it is necessary to have someone who regulates the atmosphere. The jikijitsu is the spiritual control unit. He has his own strong personal meditation practice, so he can sit quietly meditating but still have enough presence of mind to pay attention to what is happening around him. If he notices someone dozing, he might shout "Wake up!" which sends a shock wave through the zendo, helping us all to straighten our spines and pay attention to our breath. Or if there is a lot of movement and shuffling, he might shout "Be still!" Even if we aren't the ones moving, chances are that our minds are wandering off. The jikijitsu's exhortation brings us back to the moment and reminds us of our purpose.

Once I witnessed a jikijitsu, a seasoned and well-trained monk from Japan, rise from his cushion in the middle of a sit, grab a long, wooden "encouragement" stick, walk over to a sleepy student, stop directly in front of him, loudly strike the stick on the floor twice, and return to his seat. The remainder of that particular sit, for all of us in the zendo, was resoundingly and profoundly still!

While the jikijitsu is the stern father of the zendo, the jisha is the den mother, balancing the strictness that his counterpart establishes. The jisha prepares for and greets all guests, tends to the needs of the students, takes care of the sick, and organizes the cleaning of the monastery. Inherent in this job is much more than this, however, as the literal meaning of *jisha* — "to serve the saint" — implies. Jishas believe that everyone in the monastery is the incarnation of the saint Monju Bodhisattva, "he who is noble and gentle," and they treat everyone with unconditional honor, respect, warmth, and concern.

When we first encounter the foreign rituals and meditation practices of the monastery, we often experience a sense of disorientation. This can sometimes awaken an impulse to bolt from the zendo in the middle of a sit. Somehow, though, knowing that the jisha is sitting near the door, ready to care for us no matter what, gives us the strength to go on.

The jisha and the jikijitsu are the yin and yang of the zendo, embodying perfect balance and harmony.

—Myochi

Pasta Puttanesca

Forcefully seasoned, spicy puttanesca sauce is one of my all-time favorites. This vegetarian version omits the traditional anchovies. Red bell peppers add a sweetness that enhances this classic combination of flavors.

MAKES 6 TO 8 SERVINGS

¼ cup olive oil
1 medium onion, chopped
  Sea salt
2 red bell peppers, ribbed, seeded, and diced
10 garlic cloves, minced
1 28-ounce can crushed tomatoes
1 6-ounce can tomato paste
½ cup chopped kalamata olives
1 3-ounce jar capers, rinsed and drained
½ teaspoon red pepper flakes, plus more to taste
  Freshly milled black pepper
1½ pounds rigatoni, fettuccine, or linguine

1. Heat the oil in a large saucepan over medium-high heat. Add the onion and ½ teaspoon salt and sauté, stirring occasionally, until the onion begins to soften, 2 to 3 minutes. Add the peppers and garlic and sauté until the onion is translucent and the peppers soften, 5 to 8 minutes more.

2. Add the crushed tomatoes, tomato paste, olives, capers, and red pepper flakes. Reduce the heat to low, cover, and cook, stirring occasionally, until the sauce is heated through and the flavors have melded, 20 to 25 minutes. Season with black pepper and additional salt and red pepper flakes to taste.

3. Meanwhile, bring a large pot of salted water to a boil. Add the pasta and cook, stirring occasionally, until al dente, 9 to 11 minutes. Drain well. Toss the sauce with the pasta and serve.

NOTES: If possible, buy pitted kalamata olives; they save time. Green olives can be substituted. Don't try to substitute green bell peppers for the red, though; they don't add the same essence. If you have no red bell peppers, omit them.

STRUCTURE

The daily schedule of the monastery is posted on a bulletin board outside the dining room. A typical day begins at 5:00 A.M. and ends at 9:00 P.M. This schedule rarely changes, and after only a few days, the residents have no real need to refer to it, since the structure and rhythm of each day become second nature. There is always a warning bell before each new activity so that even watches become irrelevant.

This schedule is precisely followed. Nothing is ever late. No one is tardy. There is no room to dilly-dally. As Eido Roshi says, "Time is not money. Time is life."

Without fail, the meal gong is struck precisely at 7:15 A.M. for breakfast and 1:00 P.M. for lunch. Ready or not, the head cook must strike the gong at these times and serve whatever is prepared.

But sometimes it can be difficult to stay in the moment. Sitting in the zendo, wanting the sitting meditation to end, and knowing that the end will bring a delicious meal projects us into the future. At other times, though, when we are lost in the moment, the faraway sound of the meal gong announcing the imminent meal is a sweet and gentle reminder that life goes on and that we will soon be given sustenance so that it *can* go on.

The cook striking the gong after preparing food; the head monk responding to this signal and striking his bell, releasing us from one moment and leading us into the next; students and monks listening and responding by rising, retrieving bowls, and filing out of the zendo into the dining room: each of us is in the right place doing what we are meant to be doing. The movement of life within the monastery is a beautifully choreographed slice of time.

—Myochi

Classic Marinara Sauce

Many retreat group participants have asked for this recipe and its variations. This recipe is dedicated to them. Serve it with your favorite pasta, or use it in eggplant Parmesan or lasagna.

MAKES ABOUT 11 CUPS

½ cup olive oil
2 medium onions, chopped
1 teaspoon sea salt
8 whole garlic cloves, peeled
4 bay leaves
1 tablespoon dried oregano, crumbled
1 teaspoon dried basil, crumbled
1 teaspoon fennel seeds, toasted (see page 6) and ground
3 28-ounce cans crushed tomatoes
Unsweetened applesauce (optional)

1. Heat the oil in a large pot over medium-high heat. Add the onions and salt and sauté, stirring occasionally, until the onions begin to soften, about 2 minutes. Reduce the heat to medium, add the garlic, bay leaves, oregano, basil, and fennel seeds and sauté, stirring occasionally, until the onions are completely translucent and almost starting to caramelize, about 20 minutes.

2. Stir in the crushed tomatoes and bring to a boil, stirring occasionally. Reduce the heat to low and simmer for about 1 hour, stirring occasionally. Taste and correct the seasonings, adding the applesauce to taste if you prefer a sweeter sauce.

NOTE: Do not cover the pot during cooking. Whether or not you think the sauce needs the applesauce may depend on the brand of crushed tomatoes.

VARIATIONS

Toasted Fennel Marinara Sauce
MAKES ABOUT 11 CUPS

Increase the amount of toasted fennel seeds to 1 tablespoon plus 1 teaspoon and continue as directed.

Roasted Eggplant and Red Pepper Marinara Sauce

MAKES ABOUT 14 CUPS

This version goes especially well with rigatoni or eggplant Parmesan.

Roast 2 medium (1-pound) eggplants, pierced a few times with a fork, in a 400°F oven for about 1 hour, or until they collapse. Let cool, scrape the flesh into a food processor or blender, and puree until smooth. Set aside. Sauté 2 chopped red bell peppers with the onions. Continue as directed. Stir the eggplant puree into the marinara sauce after it has simmered for about 1 hour.

Asiago-Tomato Cream Sauce

MAKES ABOUT 12 CUPS

Make Classic Marinara Sauce. Just before removing it from the heat, stir in ¼ pound freshly grated Asiago cheese (about 2 cups) and ¾ cup heavy cream.

VITALITY

DISHES CONTAINING TOFU, GRAINS, AND BEANS OCCUPY THE MIDDLE, OR second, bowl. I think of this part of the meal as the center, since the food is more complex. This is where I spend the bulk of my preparation time and where I can be most creative. The middle bowl is a nourishing and substantial offering, connecting the first and third bowls. For example, a hearty curry in the second bowl links basmati rice in the first bowl with a raita in the third. These dishes are frequently the favorites of the diners.

During formal meals, it's not uncommon for students to be enticed by a dish like Almond Thai Curry and have their attention diverted as the familiar alluring aroma fills the dining room. Instead of properly concentrating on the serving bowl that is presently in front of them, they steal quick sideways glances down the table as the next bowl slowly makes its way toward them. Often, they refrain from filling their first bowl completely with rice so they can ladle extra curry into it and heap their second bowl with the curry as well. Occasionally, they will even fill their third bowl. Even those who know better have been seduced into this practice by an especially tempting dish.

—Seppo

Almond Thai Curry

The almond butter (available in gourmet or natural food stores) makes this curry a bit heavier and creamier than the traditional fiery version. The amount of Thai curry paste results in a somewhat spicy dish, though it's not blistering. If you prefer a very hot curry, add more curry paste in moderate amounts. I usually make this dish with tofu that has been frozen and then thawed, because freezing makes the tofu more absorbent, so that it soaks up the curry sauce better. Serve over a bed of rice with the raita of your choice (pages 119 and 120) on the side.

MAKES 8 TO 10 SERVINGS

¼ cup canola or corn oil
2 medium onions, halved vertically and thinly sliced
½ teaspoon sea salt
1 3-inch piece galangal root, grated (juice reserved)
2 cups Basic Vegetable Stock (page 134) or water
1 13.5-ounce can unsweetened coconut milk
½ cup almond butter, hazelnut butter, or peanut butter
2 tablespoons Thai green curry paste, plus more to taste
7 kaffir lime leaves, stems removed and discarded, ground in an electric spice grinder or very thinly shredded (see opposite page), or 1½ teaspoons grated lime zest and 1 tablespoon plus 2 teaspoons fresh lime juice
1½ pounds potatoes, peeled and cut into 1-inch cubes
4 large carrots, sliced into ½-inch-thick rounds
1 pound tofu, frozen (see opposite page), thawed, and torn into bite-size pieces, or 1 pound firm tofu, cut into 1-inch cubes
2 tablespoons tamari
Sliced almonds (optional)

1. Heat the oil in a large pot over medium-high heat. Add the onions and salt and sauté, stirring occasionally, until the onions soften and are almost translucent, about 6 minutes. Add the galangal root and any reserved juice and sauté until the onions are translucent, about 4 minutes more.

2. Meanwhile, whisk together the stock or water, coconut milk, nut butter, curry paste, and lime leaves (if using ground leaves) in a large bowl. Add the coconut mixture, lime leaves (if using shredded leaves), potatoes, and carrots to the onions and bring to a boil, stirring occasionally. Reduce the heat to low, cover, and simmer, stir-

ring occasionally, until the vegetables are tender, 35 to 45 minutes. If you prefer a thicker sauce, cook for 15 minutes more, so the starch from the potatoes can thicken the sauce.

3. Stir in the lime zest and juice (if using) and the tofu and tamari. Season to taste with more curry paste and/or tamari. Serve hot, garnished with the almonds, if using.

NOTE: Frozen galangal root is easier to grate than fresh.

TO SHRED KAFFIR LIME LEAVES: First, remove the stems, halving the leaves lengthwise. Stack 4 to 8 halves and, with a sharp knife, slice them crosswise as thinly as possible.

TO FREEZE TOFU: Place the entire package in the freezer for 2 days. To thaw, place in hot water. Periodically squeeze the tofu gently and add more hot water to bring up the temperature. Thawing will take about ½ hour.

Japanese-Style Curry

Monastery residents have dubbed this dish "curry in a hurry" because it is often served for lunch on busy Saturdays. It's a longtime favorite and a staple dish for large groups. Serve over a bed of Basmati Rice with Raisins and Walnuts (page 32) and with Beet Raita with Dill, Lime, and Honey (page 119) or Cucumber-Grape Raita with Tofu (page 120) on the side.

MAKES 4 TO 6 SERVINGS

2½ tablespoons curry powder, plus more to taste
 3 tablespoons canola or corn oil
 2 medium onions, halved vertically and thinly sliced
 1 teaspoon sea salt, plus more to taste
 1 pound portobello mushrooms (stems and caps), cut into 1-inch cubes, or 1 pound white mushrooms, halved or quartered (depending on size)
1½ pounds potatoes, cut into 1-to-1½-inch cubes
 ¼ cup plus 1 tablespoon cornstarch or potato starch (see page 67)
2½ tablespoons tamari, plus more to taste
 1 pound tofu, frozen, thawed (see page 65), and torn into bite-size pieces, or 1 pound firm tofu, cut into 1-inch cubes (optional)
 1 cup frozen peas
   Raisins (optional)
   Walnuts, toasted (see page 6) and chopped (optional)

1. Whisk the curry powder into 1 cup cold water in a small bowl and set aside.

2. Heat the oil in a large pot over medium-high heat. Add the onions and salt and sauté, stirring occasionally, until the onions are translucent, about 8 minutes.

3. Add the mushrooms and sauté until they begin to soften, about 2 minutes. Stir in the potatoes and sauté for 1 minute more. Add 4 cups cold water and the curry mixture and bring to a boil. Reduce the heat to low, cover, and simmer, stirring occasionally, until the potatoes can easily be pierced with a fork, about 20 minutes.

4. Whisk the cornstarch or potato starch with the tamari and 2 tablespoons cold water in a small bowl. Add to the curry and stir gently until the sauce thickens.

5. Gently stir in the tofu, if using, and the peas and cook until heated through, 5 to 10 minutes.

Taste and adjust the seasonings with additional curry powder, salt, and/or tamari, if desired. If you like, serve with small bowls of raisins and walnuts on the side.

NOTE: Potato starch can be found in many Asian markets and some natural food stores.

Sautéed Tofu with Spinach and Hijiki

This eclectic combination of hijiki and tofu with spinach and red bell pepper is lightly seasoned with the flavors of Asia and Latin America. Serve with your favorite rice dish.

MAKES 6 TO 8 SERVINGS

2 ounces dried hijiki (about 1 cup)
2 tablespoons canola or corn oil
1 tablespoon sesame oil
1 medium onion, diced
½ teaspoon sea salt
1 red bell pepper, ribbed, seeded, and diced
4 garlic cloves, minced
1 1-inch piece ginger, peeled and grated
1 10-ounce package frozen chopped spinach, thawed
2 large carrots, grated
¼ cup tamari
1 teaspoon Chipotle Paste (page 192) or ½ teaspoon
        cayenne pepper
3 pounds tofu (any kind), cut into ½-inch-thick slices,
        pressed (see opposite page), and cut into ½-inch
        cubes

1. Boil 4 cups water in a small saucepan. Remove from the heat, add the hijiki, cover, and let stand for 30 minutes. Drain and set aside. Discard the water.

2. Heat both oils in a large pot over medium-high heat. Add the onion and salt and sauté, stirring occasionally, until the onion is almost translucent, about 5 minutes. Add the red pepper, garlic, and ginger and sauté, stirring almost constantly, until the onion is translucent, about 3 minutes more.

3. Reduce the heat to medium and add the hijiki, spinach, and carrots. Sauté, stirring occasionally, until the carrots soften, about 15 minutes.

4. Stir in the tamari and chipotle paste or cayenne. Add the tofu, cover, and cook, stirring occasionally, until the tofu is heated through, about 10 minutes. Serve.

TO PRESS TOFU: Tofu can be pressed to drain some of its water and make it firmer. Cut a block of tofu into ½-inch-thick slices. Lay the slices on an absorbent towel, such as a kitchen towel or bath towel; do not use paper towels. Place another towel over the tofu. Put a cutting board or cookie sheet over the top towel and set a few canned goods on it to weigh it down. Don't worry about squishing the tofu. Let stand for at least 20 minutes. Check the tofu. If you'd like it to drain more, cover again and let stand longer.

Simmered Tofu in Mellow Shiitake Dashi

In this dish, chunks of soft tofu are simmered in a very light shiitake dashi, or broth. Serve with Spinach Rice (page 28) and a simple vegetable dish, such as Roasted Butternut Squash (page 104).

MAKES 4 TO 6 SERVINGS

12 dried shiitake mushrooms
3 pounds soft tofu, cut into 1-by-2-inch pieces
    (about 15 per pound)
¼ teaspoon sea salt
1 scallion, thinly sliced on the diagonal (see page 45)
    Citrus Tamari (page 199)

1. Bring 8 cups water and the mushrooms to a boil in a large saucepan. Reduce the heat to low, cover, and simmer for 1 hour. Transfer the mushrooms to a medium bowl with a slotted spoon. Strain the broth through a fine sieve or a coffee filter placed in a strainer set over a large pot to remove any dirt. Set the broth aside.

2. Thoroughly clean the mushrooms in cold water, running your fingers under the gills to remove any silt. Blot the mushrooms dry, cut off and discard the stems, and thinly slice across the caps. Set aside.

3. Bring the broth to a simmer. Gently lower the tofu into the broth and simmer over medium-low heat until the tofu is heated through, about 20 minutes. (Do not let it boil, which will fill the tofu with air holes, making it less palatable.)

4. Gently remove the tofu from the pot and divide it among individual bowls. Add the salt to the broth and pour it over the tofu, dividing it among the bowls. Divide the mushrooms and scallion among the bowls. Serve each portion with a small bowl of Citrus Tamari alongside for dipping the tofu.

THE TENZO

The tenzo is one of the officers of the monastery whose main function is to prepare the food for the monastery. But if that were all he had to do, then any kind of cook would suffice. The difference between a cook and a tenzo is that the tenzo works in the kitchen as if it were a zendo. By neatly, cleanly, silently, and punctually preparing the food, he maintains a zazen atmosphere. Even more important, he wastes nothing. For instance, suppose he uses wood for cooking. If he saves a piece of wood each day, in one year he can save three hundred sixty-five pieces. This "no-waste" practice of the tenzo applies to everything, including electricity and water.

When the tenzo is good, the rest of the sesshin goes well. If he is sloppy, the other monks find it more difficult to go on. Working behind closed doors in the kitchen, the tenzo himself remains inconspicuous, but his work is most conspicuous, most influential.

—Eido Roshi

Tofu Sashimi Platter

This refreshing dish of raw tofu served on a bed of finely shredded cabbage and carrots and accompanied by traditional sashimi condiments is served every other day during sesshin, and we always enjoy it. It's an impressive dish for a light lunch or a summer buffet. You can present it as simply or elaborately as you like. Serve with rice and a green salad tossed with Sesame-Tamari Dressing (page 122) or Ginger-Carrot Dressing (page 124).

MAKES 4 TO 6 SERVINGS

¼ medium green cabbage head, very thinly shredded (see notes)
1 large carrot, grated
1½ pounds soft tofu, preferably fresh (see notes), cut into ½-inch-thick slices and pressed, if desired (see page 69)
2 ounces sprouts, such as alfalfa, radish, or sunflower (about 2 cups)
   Thinly sliced scallions (see page 45; optional)
   Tamari or Citrus Tamari (page 199)
   Peeled and grated fresh or pickled ginger (see page 22; optional)
   Wasabi paste (see page 45; optional)

Scatter the cabbage and carrot on a platter, forming a bed for the tofu. Arrange the tofu around the outside of the platter, overlapping the slices slightly so that they look like a circle of fallen dominoes. Place the sprouts in the center of the platter. Sprinkle the tofu with the scallions. Serve with the tamari or citrus tamari and the ginger and wasabi, if using.

NOTES: This platter can be made in advance, covered with plastic, and stored in the refrigerator for a few hours. A quick spritz with a water mister just before serving will make the tofu glisten. Since the tofu is served raw and stands mostly on its own, its purity is essential to the success of this dish. The fresher the tofu, the better. Buy fresh tofu in Asian markets.

TO SHRED CABBAGE THINLY: Peel the outer leaves from the head, trying not to tear them. (The leaves toward the heart of the cabbage are too thick for this recipe.) Cut the large center stems from the leaves. Stack 2 or 3 leaves and roll them up as tightly as possible in the direction of the natural curl of the leaves. Using a very sharp knife, slice across the cabbage as thinly as you can, making paper-thin slices.

THE TEN PRECEPTS OF BUDDHISM

I will be reverential and mindful with all life;
I will not be violent, nor will I kill.

I will respect others' property;
I will not steal.

I will be conscious and loving in my relationships;
I will not give way to lust.

I will honor honesty and truth;
I will not deceive.

I will exercise proper care of my body and mind;
I will not be gluttonous nor abuse intoxicants.

I will remember that silence is precious;
I will not gossip or engage in frivolous conversation.

I will be humble;
I will not praise myself and judge others.

I will be grateful for my life;
I will not covet, envy, or be jealous.

I will keep my mind always calm and at peace;
I will not give way to anger.

I will esteem the Three Treasures: Buddha, dharma, and sangha.
I will not defame them.

Asian-Style Tortilla Rolls

When I'm pressed for time, I often forgo the tortillas, toss the filling with hoisin sauce, and serve it in a bowl. The hoisin makes the filling taste like the traditional Chinese mu-shu filling. Serve with rice.

MAKES 4 TO 6 SERVINGS

1 tablespoon sesame oil

1 tablespoon canola or corn oil

½ medium onion, diced

½ teaspoon sea salt

8 garlic cloves, minced

1 3-inch piece ginger, peeled and grated

4 large carrots, minced or cut into 1-inch rounds and pulsed in a food processor

1 cup diced green cabbage

1 10-ounce package frozen chopped spinach, thawed

5 kaffir lime leaves, stems removed, ground in an electric spice grinder or very thinly shredded (see page 65), or 1 teaspoon grated lime zest and 1 tablespoon plus 1 teaspoon fresh lime juice

8 ounces soft tofu, mashed

½ cup walnuts, toasted (see page 6) and ground

1 tablespoon plus 1 teaspoon tamari

Shredded green cabbage, for lining the baking pan (see opposite page)

12 6-inch or eight 8-inch whole wheat tortillas

2 tablespoons hoisin sauce mixed with 2 tablespoons water (optional)

1. Heat both oils in a large skillet over medium-high heat. Add the onion and salt and sauté, stirring occasionally, until the onion is almost translucent, about 5 minutes. Reduce the heat to medium, add the garlic and ginger, and sauté, stirring, until the onion is translucent and the garlic softens, about 3 minutes more.

2. Increase the heat to medium-high, add the carrots, spinach, diced cabbage, and lime leaves (if using shredded leaves). Cook, stirring frequently, until the carrots are tender and the cabbage remains a bit crunchy, about 15 minutes.

3. Add the tofu and walnuts and cook until heated through, about 5 minutes. Stir in the tamari and lime leaves (if using ground leaves) or zest and juice. Remove from the heat.

4. Preheat the oven to 350°F. Place a thin bed of shredded cabbage in a 9-x-13-inch baking dish, or lightly coat the dish with spray, oil, or butter. Spread ⅓ cup of filling along the center of each 6-inch tortilla (use ½ cup each for 8-inch tortillas), leaving a margin of ½ inch at each end. Spread 1 teaspoon of the hoisin sauce, if using, over the vegetables. Fold the sides over the filling, forming a burrito shape. Place seam side down in the baking dish. Continue filling the remaining tortillas in the same way. Cover the dish with foil and bake until heated through, 15 to 20 minutes. Gently lift out the tortilla rolls with a spatula and serve.

NOTES: The cabbage keeps the tortillas from touching the bottom of the pan, so they stay soft, and releases moisture to help steam them.

TO PREPARE IN ADVANCE: The filling can be made in advance and refrigerated. The tortilla rolls can be assembled and refrigerated or individually wrapped and frozen. Double the recipe and make extras to have on hand in the freezer when you want a quick meal. To reheat, place the frozen tortilla rolls, wrapped in foil, in a preheated 350°F oven for about 45 minutes.

Sesame Tofu (Gomadofu)

In traditional Japanese temple cuisine, this is considered the richest of guest foods. Although labor-intensive, it's well worth the time and energy. Sesame Tofu, or *gomadofu*, as it is called in Japanese, is actually not tofu at all. It is a sesame-flavored, tofu-textured delicacy made from homemade sesame milk that has been thickened with kudzu.

MAKES 6 TO 8 SERVINGS

2 cups white or brown sesame seeds, toasted (see page 6)

1 heaping cup kudzu

4 cups fresh salad greens (optional)

Wasabi paste (see page 45)

Tamari

1. Place the sesame seeds and 4 cups water in a blender and puree until the seeds are ground as finely as possible, about 5 minutes. Strain through a fine sieve into a large saucepan, pressing down on the solids with a spatula to extract all the liquid. Discard the solids.

2. Add the kudzu and stir it in with your hands; do not use a spoon. The kudzu will sink to the bottom of the pan, and when you can no longer feel any grittiness, it is completely dissolved.

3. Rinse a 5-x-9-inch loaf pan with cold water. Dump out any excess, but do not towel dry. Set aside.

4. Set the sesame mixture over medium-high heat and cook, stirring constantly with a heatproof rubber spatula, until it pulls away from the sides of the pan, about 10 minutes. At first, the consistency will be thick and lumpy, but as you continue stirring, it will become smooth, satiny, and thick.

5. Remove from the heat and stir constantly for 2 minutes more. Scrape the sesame mixture into the rinsed loaf pan and spread it as well as you can. Slap it with the spatula or a wooden spoon briskly and loudly, about a dozen times. This will help remove air bubbles and shape it into the form of the loaf pan.

6. Place the loaf pan in a cold water bath and fill the pan with cold water as well. (The *gomadofu* is too dense to absorb the water.) Let

stand for about 1 hour, changing the water every 15 minutes. The *gomadofu* can be stored in the refrigerator at this point for up to 1½ days. (Store it in the loaf pan and keep the surface covered with water.)

7. Turn out the loaf of *gomadofu* onto a wet cutting board. Slice it in half lengthwise, then slice it into thin squares. The *gomadofu* is easiest to handle if you cut it with a wet knife and wet the squares with your fingertips after cutting them.

8. Serve on a bed of salad greens, if desired, or on a wet platter, with the wasabi and tamari on the side.

Herbed Sesame Polenta with Roasted Vegetables

This polenta is cooked with sesame oil, garlic, and herbs, then topped with colorful roasted Mediterranean vegetables. It can be brought to the table hot or made in advance and served at room temperature.

MAKES 6 TO 8 SERVINGS

SESAME POLENTA

- 1 tablespoon sesame oil
- 2 garlic cloves, minced
- 7 cups Basic Vegetable Stock (page 134) or water
- 1 tablespoon plus 1 teaspoon tamari
- 2 cups coarse cornmeal
- ¾ teaspoon dried sage, crumbled
- ½ teaspoon dried oregano, crumbled
- 2 tablespoons sesame seeds, toasted (see page 6)

ROASTED VEGETABLES

- 1 large eggplant (about 1 pound), peeled and cut into 1-inch cubes
- 1 medium red onion, cut vertically into eighths
- 3 tablespoons olive oil
- 1 red bell pepper, ribbed, seeded, and cut into 1-inch pieces
- 1 large zucchini, trimmed, halved lengthwise, and cut into ½-inch-thick slices
- 2 medium tomatoes, coarsely chopped
- 10–12 ounces white mushrooms, cut into ¼-inch-thick slices

- ½ cup kalamata or other black olives, pitted and sliced
- 1 tablespoon sesame seeds, toasted (see page 6)

1. SESAME POLENTA: Heat the oil in a large saucepan over medium-low heat. Add the garlic and sauté, stirring constantly, until it is fragrant and begins to soften, about 3 minutes; do not let it stick to the pan or brown. Add the stock or water and tamari, increase the heat to high, and bring to a boil. Reduce the heat to medium-low and slowly add the cornmeal, whisking continuously to avoid lumps.

Once the cornmeal has thickened, add the sage and oregano and cook, stirring almost constantly, until the polenta thickens and starts to pull away from the sides of the pan, 20 to 25 minutes. Spread the polenta evenly onto a large serving platter or into a 9-x-11-inch baking dish. Sprinkle with the sesame seeds.

2. ROASTED VEGETABLES: Preheat the oven to 400°F and coat a baking sheet with spray, oil, or butter. Toss the eggplant and onion thoroughly with the olive oil in a large bowl. Place the eggplant and onion on the baking sheet and roast for 10 minutes. Add the bell pepper, toss quickly with a spatula, and roast for 5 minutes more. Toss in the zucchini and roast for 5 minutes more. Add the tomatoes, toss, and roast for 5 minutes more. Toss in the mushrooms and roast for 5 minutes.

3. Spread the roasted vegetables over the polenta. Sprinkle the olives and sesame seeds over the vegetables and serve.

NOTE: To serve both the polenta and the vegetables hot, prepare all the vegetables before you start to cook the polenta and toss the eggplant and onion with the olive oil. Begin roasting the vegetables about 10 minutes after the polenta has started. This will give the polenta just enough time to set without cooling substantially. As you stir the polenta almost constantly (for at least 45 seconds of every minute), roast the vegetables. Be mindful!

Sesame Crepes with Portobello Mushrooms in Port Cream Sauce

These exquisite crepes were inspired by Karen Hubert Allison's book *The Vegetarian Compass*, though I have taken liberties with her original recipe. These crepes are always a huge success. They are perfect for a dinner party or any time you want to serve an impressive and elegant main dish. Serve with Nondairy Mashed Potatoes (page 102), Quinoa-Sunflower Stuffing (page 88), Garden Brown Sauce (page 200), Roasted Butternut Squash (page 104), and Raspberry-Glazed Beets (page 94).

MAKES 6 TO 8 CREPES

SESAME CREPES

- ½ cup whole wheat pastry flour
- ½ cup milk, soy milk, or rice milk
- 2 large eggs
- 3 tablespoons sesame seeds, toasted (see page 6)
- 1 tablespoon sesame or olive oil, plus more for the griddle
- 1 teaspoon maple syrup
- ½ teaspoon sea salt

PORTOBELLO FILLING

- 2 tablespoons olive oil
- ½ medium onion, minced
- 1 pound portobello mushrooms, cut into julienne pieces
- ¼ cup port
- ½ cup Basic Vegetable Stock (page 134) or water
- 3 tablespoons heavy cream
- 1 teaspoon freshly grated nutmeg
  Dab Chipotle Paste (page 192) or pinch cayenne pepper
  Sea salt and freshly milled black pepper

1. SESAME CREPES: Mix all the ingredients and 2 tablespoons water in a blender or food processor. Lightly brush a griddle or skillet set over medium heat with sesame or olive oil. Using about 3 tablespoons batter for each crepe, pour the batter onto the griddle or into the skillet and immediately tilt the pan to spread it into a thin, even layer. Cook for 1 minute, or until the top is set. Flip carefully with a spatula and your fingers and cook the other side for about 15 seconds, or until lightly browned. Brush the pan with oil as needed, about every 2 or 3 crepes. Stack the finished crepes directly on top of each other and cover with a kitchen towel. The crepes can be made in advance, wrapped in plastic, and refrigerated for several days.

2. PORTOBELLO FILLING: Heat the oil in a skillet over medium-high heat. Sauté the onion, stirring occasionally, until almost translucent, about 5 minutes. Add the mushrooms and sauté, stirring occasionally, until they soften, darken in color, and begin to exude their juices, about 5 minutes more. Pour in the port and scrape up browned bits from the bottom of the pan with a spatula. Add the stock or water and cream and boil until slightly thickened, about 3 minutes. Add the nutmeg, chipotle paste or cayenne, and salt and pepper to taste. The filling can be made in advance and stored for 1 to 2 days in the refrigerator.

3. To assemble the crepes, spread about ¼ cup filling down the center of each crepe and roll up. Arrange seam side down on a platter and serve warm.

NOTES: You can roll the crepes a few hours before serving and reheat them briefly on a baking sheet in a 350°F oven. Cover the baking sheet lightly with shredded cabbage. (The cabbage keeps the bottom of the tortillas soft and releases moisture to help steam them.) Place the rolled crepes on the cabbage and wrap the pan tightly with foil. Heat for about 15 minutes, or until warmed through. Serve immediately.

Quinoa Vegetable Stew

Quinoa, a delicate-tasting grain, has long been a staple in South American cooking. It packs more protein than any other grain, and it is complete protein. In this light stew, quinoa combines with tender vegetables and Mexican spices. Serve with salad and crusty bread.

MAKES 4 TO 6 SERVINGS

½ cup quinoa, rinsed well and drained
2 tablespoons olive oil
1 medium onion, chopped
¼ teaspoon sea salt, plus more to taste
1 large carrot, chopped
2 garlic cloves, minced
1 14.5-ounce can whole tomatoes, coarsely chopped, juice reserved
¾ cup Basic Vegetable Stock (page 134) or water
1 red bell pepper, ribbed, seeded, and diced
1 small zucchini, trimmed and cubed
½ cup fresh or frozen corn kernels
½ cup fresh or frozen peas
2 teaspoons ground cumin
1 teaspoon ground coriander
1 teaspoon dried oregano, crumbled
½ teaspoon chili powder
  Pinch cayenne pepper
1 tablespoon fresh lemon juice
  Freshly milled black pepper
  Grated cheddar or Monterey Jack cheese (optional)
  Chopped fresh cilantro (optional)

1. Bring 1 cup water to a boil in a small saucepan. Add the quinoa, reduce the heat to very low, cover, and simmer until the water is completely absorbed and the quinoa is tender, 15 to 20 minutes.

2. Meanwhile, heat the oil in a large saucepan over medium-high heat. Add the onion and salt and sauté, stirring occasionally, until the onion begins to soften, about 2 minutes. Stir in the carrot and garlic, cover, and cook, stirring occasionally, until the carrot is crisp-tender, about 6 minutes more.

3. Add the tomatoes and their juice, vegetable stock or water, bell pepper, zucchini, corn, peas, cumin, coriander, oregano, chili powder, and cayenne. Bring to a boil, cover, reduce the heat to low, and simmer until the vegetables are cooked to the desired doneness, 10 to 15 minutes. Stir in the quinoa and lemon juice and season with salt and pepper to taste. Serve hot, garnished with the cheese and/or a sprinkling of cilantro, if desired.

VARIATIONS

Spicy Quinoa Stew

Add ½ to 1 fresh minced jalapeño pepper when you add the tomatoes and stock. Half a jalapeño will make the stew spicy. A whole jalapeño will make it very spicy.

Hearty Quinoa Stew

You can easily turn this stew into a hearty one-dish meal by adding 1 to 2 cups cooked pinto beans or chickpeas 5 minutes after you add the tomatoes.

Sweet Potato– Walnut Burritos

These burritos were originally created to use up leftover sweet potatoes and lentils. We liked them so much that we now cook sweet potatoes and lentils especially for this dish. Sour cream and/or salsa make nice accompaniments, along with Brown Rice with Quinoa (page 26). Start the grains and prepare the salad while the lentils and sweet potatoes cook. The burritos can be prepared up to a few hours in advance.

MAKES 4 TO 6 SERVINGS

½ cup green lentils or split peas, sorted, rinsed well, and drained
1 large sweet potato (about 1 pound), peeled and cut into 1-inch cubes
2 tablespoons olive oil
1 medium onion, chopped
½ teaspoon sea salt
2 garlic cloves, minced
1½ teaspoons chili powder
½ teaspoon ground cumin
½ teaspoon ground coriander
½ teaspoon Chipotle Paste (page 192) or ¼ teaspoon cayenne pepper, or more to taste
½ cup grated cheddar or Monterey Jack cheese
¾ cup walnuts, toasted (see page 6) and ground or chopped, if desired
¾ cup canned crushed tomatoes

Shredded green cabbage, for lining the baking pan (see page 75; optional)
6 8-inch flour tortillas
1 large tomato, halved and thinly sliced
½ cup grated cheddar or Monterey Jack cheese
Chopped fresh cilantro or parsley (optional)

1. Place the lentils or split peas and 1⅓ cups water for lentils or 1½ cups water for peas in a medium saucepan and bring to a boil. Reduce the heat to low, cover, and simmer until tender yet firm, 25 to 35 minutes for lentils, 1 hour and 15 minutes for peas. Drain and set aside.

2. Place the sweet potato in a medium saucepan with just enough water to cover. Bring to a boil, reduce the heat to low, cover, and simmer until the cubes are soft but still hold their shape, about 20 minutes. Drain and mash them in a large bowl. Set aside.

3. Heat the oil in a large skillet over medium-high heat. Add the onion and salt and sauté, stirring occasionally, until the onion begins to soften, about 2 minutes. Reduce the heat to medium and stir in the garlic, chili powder, cumin, coriander, and chipotle paste or cayenne. Sauté until the onion is translucent, about 6 minutes more. Add the onion mixture, lentils or split peas, ½ cup of the cheese, the walnuts, and crushed tomatoes to the mashed sweet potato and mix well.

4. TO ASSEMBLE AND BAKE THE BURRITOS: Preheat the oven to 350°F. Place a thin bed of shredded cabbage in a 9-x-13-inch baking dish, if desired, or lightly coat the dish with spray, oil, or butter. Fill a tortilla with about one-sixth of the filling and roll it securely. Place it seam side down in the baking dish. Continue with the remaining tortillas. Cover the dish tightly with foil. (You can prepare the burritos 1 to 2 hours ahead up to this point and store at room temperature.) Bake for 30 minutes, or until heated through.

5. Remove the foil from the baking dish. Place 1 or 2 tomato slices on each burrito. Sprinkle the remaining ½ cup cheese over them and return the dish to the oven for a few minutes to melt it. Place the burritos on a platter and sprinkle with the cilantro or parsley, if desired. Serve immediately.

NOTES: There are two different ways to assemble the burritos. If you're in a hurry, as I usually am, you can mix all the ingredients together in a large bowl, as the instructions direct, then fill the tortillas. Or, for a more elegant presentation, keep the ingredients separate and layer them when you assemble each burrito, starting with the sweet potato, then the lentils or split peas, onion mixture, crushed tomatoes, walnuts, and cheese.

Leftover burritos, individually wrapped in foil and frozen, make for an easy meal when you are in a hurry and don't have time to fuss in the kitchen. To reheat frozen burritos, wrap in foil and place in a preheated 350°F oven for about 45 minutes.

Quinoa-Mushroom Nut Loaf

This savory loaf goes perfectly with Nondairy Mashed Potatoes (page 102) and Garden Brown Sauce (page 200), with a vegetable on the side. It can be made up to two days in advance and refrigerated in the loaf pan. Leftovers, which are rare, make a good "meat loaf" sandwich.

MAKES ONE 5-X-9-INCH LOAF, 6 TO 8 SERVINGS

1 cup quinoa, rinsed well and drained
2 tablespoons olive oil
2 large celery ribs, diced
1 medium onion, diced
1½ teaspoons sea salt
10–12 ounces white mushrooms, sliced
1½ cups wheat germ, toasted (see page 6)
1 cup walnuts, toasted (see page 6) and ground
½ cup whole wheat bread crumbs
1 large egg, lightly whisked
1 tablespoon dried sage, crumbled
2 teaspoons dried thyme, crumbled
1 teaspoon dried rosemary, crumbled
Freshly milled black pepper

1. Bring 2 cups water to a boil in a medium saucepan. Add the quinoa, reduce the heat to very low, cover, and simmer until the water is completely absorbed and the quinoa is tender, 15 to 20 minutes. Remove from the heat, cover, and set aside.

2. Preheat the oven to 350°F and generously coat a 5-x-9-inch loaf pan with spray, oil, or butter.

3. Heat the olive oil in a large skillet over medium-high heat. Add the celery, onion, and salt and sauté, stirring occasionally, until the onion is almost translucent, about 5 minutes. Add the mushrooms and sauté, stirring occasionally, until all the juices have evaporated and the vegetables just begin to stick to the pan. Transfer to a large bowl.

4. Add the quinoa and remaining ingredients. Mix well with your hands. Pack the mixture tightly into the loaf pan.

5. Bake for about 1 hour, or until the top is toasty brown. Let cool for 10 minutes, loosen the sides with a spatula, and carefully flip the nut loaf onto a serving platter. Slice carefully. Serve.

BEING ZAZEN

Some forty-five-minute sits seem to go by in a flash; others seem to drag on endlessly. The variety of experiences that we have sitting on our black cushions mirrors our lives off the cushion. No two sits are the same. No two moments are identical. This fact of life — that everything changes and nothing is permanent — is driven home to us each time we sit, if we are open to learning the lesson. Yet somehow, even once we've learned it (and usually it's the hard, painful way), we tend to slip readily into old habits and forgetfulness. It's not easy to pay constant attention to every detail of life, especially when we first start on this zazen path. And when we come to it with a lifetime of lazy habits, we are especially resistant. But, little by little, the more we sit zazen, the more we become zazen, and it becomes our way of life. Our lazy, daydreaming-being becomes an alert being-being, tuned in to every precious moment.

The first zazen instruction is to keep your eyes open and simply begin counting your breaths. Inhale, exhale: one. Inhale, exhale: two. Count up to ten, and begin again. Simple. But try it for yourself and you'll know that it's not so easy.

Legs and feet cramp or fall asleep, hands become stiff, back and shoulder muscles tense, breathing becomes shallow or stops altogether, the mind races, eyes close, and dreams interfere with concentration. Every little noise is a disturbance, every little pain creates havoc, every thought cries out for release. But then there are those moments that keep us returning to the cushion: moments that contain pure joy, pure understanding, pure freedom. And so we keep at it, training our bodies and minds to relax into themselves and just be. And then we are not only doing zazen, we are being zazen. And being zazen is what everything else is about: so we can be zazen even when we are not doing zazen.

—Myochi

Quinoa-Sunflower Stuffing

This protein-packed, savory stuffing is great for the holidays. It can be used to stuff zucchini, eggplant, acorn squash, and many other vegetables. It doesn't need a sauce, but the flavors work well with Garden Brown Sauce (page 200).

MAKES 6 TO 8 SERVINGS

3 tablespoons canola or corn oil
1 medium onion, diced
1 teaspoon sea salt
3 large celery ribs, chopped
10–12 ounces mushrooms, cut into ¼-inch-thick slices
2 large carrots, grated
3 garlic cloves, minced
2 teaspoons dried sage, crumbled
1 teaspoon dried basil, crumbled
½ teaspoon ground fennel seeds
½ teaspoon dried oregano, crumbled
½ teaspoon dried thyme, crumbled
¾ cup quinoa, rinsed well and drained
1 tablespoon tamari
1 cup sunflower seeds, toasted (see page 6) and ground

1. Heat the oil in a large saucepan over medium-high heat. Add the onion and salt and sauté, stirring occasionally, until the onion begins to soften, about 2 minutes. Add the celery and sauté until it is bright and tender, about 3 minutes more. Add the mushrooms, carrots, garlic, sage, basil, fennel seeds, oregano, and thyme and sauté until the mushrooms and carrots soften and most of the juices have evaporated, about 10 minutes.

2. Add 1½ cups cold water, the quinoa, and tamari and bring to a boil. Reduce the heat to very low, cover, and simmer until the water is completely absorbed and the quinoa is tender, 15 to 20 minutes. Stir in the sunflower seeds and serve immediately.

VARIATION
Quinoa-Cashew Stuffing
Substitute 1¼ cups unsalted cashews, toasted (see page 6) and ground, for the sunflower seeds.

Gingery Adzuki Beans with Spinach

Ginger and tamari are wonderful complements to adzuki beans and spinach. Serve with a simple grain for a complete meal.

MAKES 4 TO 6 SERVINGS

½ cup adzuki beans, sorted, rinsed well, and drained
1 ¾-inch piece ginger, peeled and grated
1 10-ounce package frozen chopped spinach, thawed
1½–2 tablespoons tamari
   Sea salt (optional)

1. Place the beans in a large saucepan with enough cold water to cover them by a few inches. Bring to a boil, then boil for 3 to 5 minutes. Remove from the heat, cover, and let stand for 1 hour. (Alternatively, if you have the time, you can soak the beans at room temperature for at least 4 hours or overnight.) Rinse the beans thoroughly.

2. Place the beans, ginger, and 1 cup cold water in a large saucepan and bring to a boil. Reduce the heat to low, cover, and simmer until the beans are tender but not mushy, 30 to 40 minutes.

3. Stir in the spinach, cover, and cook for about 10 minutes, or until heated through. Add 1½ tablespoons of the tamari and season to taste with salt, if using, and/or additional tamari. Serve.

VEGETABLE

ABOUT A MILE DOWN THE DIRT ROAD THAT SERVES AS OUR DRIVEWAY, halfway to the gatehouse, is a one-acre plot of land alongside Beecher Stream that serves as our garden. It is surrounded by a rickety, fifteen-foot-tall, patchwork wire fence. While the fence successfully deters the deer, it is questionable whether it keeps out any other wildlife.

There are several factors that limit the selection of vegetables that will successfully grow at Dai Bosatsu. Because we are at high altitude and the winters are long, we cannot even begin to work the earth until May. Thus, the growing season is short. In addition, we try to restrict our crops to those that are expensive and hard to find in the market.

After years of experience working within these parameters, we have come to some decisions about what will grow and what is worth our time and personpower. The appointed gardener works closely with me in the early spring when choosing seeds. Herbs such as basil and shiso, gourmet lettuces such as arugula and radicchio, hearty greens such as collards and kale, and winter squashes such as pumpkins are regular residents in our garden and fare well.

The responsibility for planting and maintaining the garden is assigned to one resident each year. During the early season, though, when there is much working of the land, the gardener receives a lot of assistance from the other residents. Gardening for the monastery, like cooking, is an all-consuming practice and requires much invisible thought and planning. To present the cooks with an overflowing bowl of vibrant, fresh greens, watch as it is served, and see everybody heartily indulging makes the labor seem worthwhile.

—Seppo

Asparagus with Lime and Tamari

Fresh lime juice and tamari add a hint of seasoning to steamed asparagus spears without overpowering their brilliant flavor. Arrange the asparagus whole on a serving platter for an elegant presentation, or slice and serve in a bowl.

MAKES 2 TO 4 SERVINGS

1 tablespoon fresh lime juice
1½ teaspoons tamari
¼ teaspoon rice vinegar
1 pound fresh asparagus, 1 inch trimmed off the base
    and, if the stalks are thicker than a pencil, peeled

1. Whisk together the lime juice, tamari, and vinegar in a small bowl and set aside.

2. Steam the asparagus until tender but not soggy, just until a knife can pierce the thick part of the stalk, 8 to 12 minutes. Immediately remove from the heat.

3. Arrange the asparagus on a serving platter. Sprinkle the lime juice mixture over them with a spoon and serve immediately.

VARIATIONS
The asparagus can be sliced into 2-inch lengths, steamed, and tossed with the dressing. (This is how it would be served when using jihatsu bowls.) It can also be made in advance, refrigerated, and served as a cold salad.

THE MOUNTAIN

As we make our way up the road to
the monastery, it's easy to believe the
lore that this mountain was once a
Native American healing ground.
The Beaverkill River rushes past,
cleansing and purifying. This
stream, the quiet stillness, the
hushed complacency of the mountain, and the deer that cross our path
slowly work their magic as we
ascend.

   And though the going is slower in
winter, it's well worth the extra time.
Ice drips off tree limbs and rock
walls and anything else that's
unmoving and upright. Shades of
white and gray and purple dance
with each other until all colors of
the spectrum make an appearance.
And then, with the first loud rush of
winter's thaw, the sound is turned up
a few notches as spring bursts forth.
The birds return, the slumbering
mountain wakes to new life, and the
night sky screams with silver stars. A
sequined blanket wraps the place in
an intimate and yet boundless skin
of energy.

—Myochi

Raspberry-Glazed Beets

These succulent glazed beets are a nice contrast to a hot and spicy dish and are versatile enough to serve for any occasion, from a simple lunch to an elaborate dinner. Serve hot, cold, or at room temperature.

MAKES 4 TO 6 SERVINGS

¼ cup plus 2 tablespoons mirin
2 tablespoons raspberry vinegar
1 tablespoon extra-virgin olive oil
1½ pounds beets (4 beets, each 2½ to 3 inches in diameter), peeled, halved vertically, and thinly sliced

1. Whisk the mirin and vinegar in a small bowl and set aside.

2. Heat the oil in a large skillet over medium-high heat. Add the beets and toss gently to coat with the oil. Cover and cook for 2 to 3 minutes. Stir, cover, and cook for 3 minutes more; stir again. Continue until the beets are cooked to the desired doneness, 15 to 20 minutes.

3. Increase the heat to high, add the mirin mixture, and cook, stirring frequently, until the liquid becomes a glossy glaze, about 2 minutes. Serve.

NOTE: The cooking time will depend on how thickly the beets are sliced. Thinly sliced beets will need less time than thicker ones, so slice them as thin as possible.

Sautéed Beets and Hijiki

In this nutritious side dish, grated beets are mixed with black hijiki for a stunning color combination. This is a subtle way to introduce sea vegetables to first-timers. For a wholesome meal with an Asian flair, serve with Shiitake Rice (page 27) and Gingery Adzuki Beans with Spinach (page 89).

MAKES 4 TO 6 SERVINGS

2 cups apple juice
1 ounce dried hijiki (about ½ cup)
1½ teaspoons sesame oil
1½ teaspoons canola or corn oil
1 pound beets (2 or 3 beets, each 2½ to 3 inches in diameter), peeled and grated
1 teaspoon tamari
¼ teaspoon sea salt
Pinch ground cinnamon

1. Bring the apple juice to a boil in a small saucepan. Remove from the heat, stir in the hijiki, cover, and let stand for 30 minutes. Drain and set aside; discard the apple juice.

2. Heat both oils in a large skillet over medium-high heat. Add the beets and sauté, stirring occasionally, until tender, about 10 minutes. Add the hijiki and sauté until heated through, about 3 minutes. Stir in the tamari, salt, and cinnamon and serve hot, cold, or at room temperature.

Sautéed Hijiki with Vegetables

Richard Pierce of the Whole Foods Project in New York City first showed me how to prepare hijiki this way. Sautéing the hijiki gives it a delicious nutty flavor that goes well with the vegetables. Serve with Tofu Sashimi Platter (page 72), or add a bit more mirin to give it a slightly sweet edge and try it alongside a spicy dish, such as Almond Thai Curry (page 64).

MAKES 4 TO 6 SERVINGS

2 ounces dried hijiki (about 1 cup)
2 tablespoons sesame oil
1 tablespoon canola or corn oil
1 medium onion, chopped
¼ teaspoon sea salt
3 large carrots, grated
¼ medium green cabbage head, thinly shredded (about 2 cups; see page 72)
2 tablespoons tamari
2 tablespoons sake
2 tablespoons mirin

1. Bring 3 cups water to a boil in a medium saucepan. Remove from the heat, add the hijiki, cover, and let stand for 30 minutes. Drain and set aside.

2. Heat both oils in a large skillet over medium-high heat. Add the onion and salt and sauté, stirring occasionally, until the onion is translucent, about 7 minutes. Reduce the heat to medium and add the hijiki, carrots, cabbage, tamari, sake, and mirin. Cook, stirring occasionally, until the vegetables start to stick to the bottom of the skillet and the carrots and cabbage have been darkened by the hijiki, about 35 minutes. Serve hot, cold, or at room temperature.

Green Beans with Orange and Dill

This distinctive side dish is a refreshing accompaniment to any main course, but it complements spicy dishes especially well. It also makes a cool salad for a hot summer day.

MAKES 4 TO 6 SERVINGS

¾ pound green beans, trimmed and cut into bite-size pieces
1 tablespoon canola or corn oil
  Grated zest of 1 large orange
  Juice of 1 large orange
2 tablespoons chopped fresh dill
  Sea salt and freshly milled black pepper

1. Steam the green beans until crisp-tender, 6 to 8 minutes. Drain in a colander.

2. Heat the oil in a large skillet over medium-high heat. Add the green beans and toss until coated with the oil and heated through, 3 to 5 minutes. Remove from the heat and stir in the orange zest, juice, and dill. Season with salt and pepper to taste and serve immediately.

VARIATION

Zesty Cool Green Bean Salad
Following the directions in the recipe, steam the green beans. Immediately after removing them from the heat, shock them in cold water and drain thoroughly in a colander. Omit the sautéing process. Whisk together the oil, zest, juice, dill, and 1 teaspoon rice vinegar (optional) in a small bowl. Toss the beans with the dressing. Season with salt and pepper to taste. Chill and toss again before serving.

Sautéed Kale with Soft Tofu

This tasty combination of kale and tofu provides a protein and a hearty vegetable in the same dish. Miso and a few simple seasonings give the tofu a cheeselike flavor — a perfect complement to the assertive taste of the kale.

MAKES 4 TO 6 SERVINGS

1 pound soft tofu, mashed
2 tablespoons white miso
1 tablespoon plus 1 teaspoon olive oil
4 garlic cloves, minced
1¼ teaspoons sea salt
8 cups packed kale leaves, large ribs removed, leaves cut into bite-size pieces
2 teaspoons fresh lemon juice

1. Mash the tofu and miso together in a medium bowl. Set aside.

2. Heat the olive oil in a large skillet over medium-low heat. Add the garlic and ½ teaspoon of the salt and sauté, stirring occasionally, until the garlic softens but is not browned, about 5 minutes.

3. Add the tofu mixture and ½ teaspoon of the salt and sauté, stirring occasionally, for 5 minutes more.

4. Add the kale and mix gently with the tofu mixture. (It's not necessary to combine them thoroughly at this point.) Cover and cook, stirring occasionally, until the kale is bright green and tender, 8 to 10 minutes. Add the lemon juice and the remaining ¼ teaspoon salt and stir well. Serve.

KINHIN

The jikijitsu, who is the head monk of the zendo, strikes his bell. At this sound, we all stand in front of our cushions ready for the next signal, ready for kinhin. *Kinhin* is walking meditation, and it is usually done slowly between periods of sitting meditation. It is meant to release our bodies from the tension of sitting still, yet it is not exactly a break from meditation but rather another form of it. We are expected to maintain our concentration during this five- or ten-minute period of walking.

The first kinhin of the day, however, is hardly contemplative or meditative, but it certainly requires concentration. And it is fast. Depending on who leads it, it can range from a brisk walk to a slow jog to a virtual run. One must be sure to keep up, leaving no large gaps. We jog around the zendo in the surrounding corridor. Then, weather permitting, we move to the deck outside. Although the temperature in the zendo is always cooler than in the rest of the monastery to encourage wakefulness during zazen, it can be hazardous to wear socks for this morning exercise because the floors are slippery.

This period of fast kinhin accomplishes a few things. It wakes us up, gets our blood moving, prepares our bodies for sitting still, and opens our lungs and diaphragms for the chanting and sitting periods that follow. It throws us into the day, reminding us that every minute is precious and that all we need to do is be alert for the magical moments of life.

—Myochi

Broccoli Rabe with Ginger, Honey, and Lemon

Broccoli rabe with an adventurous Asian twist makes a welcome accompaniment for almost any main dish.

MAKES 2 TO 4 SERVINGS

2 tablespoons olive oil
1 2-inch piece ginger, peeled and grated
1 tablespoon plus 1 teaspoon fresh lemon juice
1 tablespoon honey
1 pound broccoli rabe, 1 inch trimmed off the base of the stems, cut into 1½-inch pieces
1 tablespoon sea salt, plus more to taste
Freshly milled black pepper

1. Heat the oil in a large skillet over medium heat. Add the ginger and sauté until fragrant, about 2 minutes. Stir in the lemon juice and honey, remove from the heat, and set aside.

2. Bring 1½ gallons water to a boil. Add the broccoli rabe and salt and cook until tender, 1 to 2 minutes. Drain well.

3. Add the broccoli rabe to the lemon mixture and toss well. Season with salt and pepper to taste and serve.

Savory Whipped Sweet Potatoes with Ribbons of Collard Greens

Here's a scrumptious side dish worthy of any holiday table. A dusting of cayenne charms extra flavor out of the sweet potatoes without lending a trace of spiciness. This dish can be prepared a few hours or a few days in advance, stored in the refrigerator, and reheated in the oven just before serving. These potatoes are so sweet and flavorful that they need no butter.

MAKES 6 TO 8 SERVINGS

4 pounds sweet potatoes (approximately 4 large or 5 medium potatoes), pierced a few times with a fork
1 teaspoon canola or corn oil
1 cup packed collard green leaves, large ribs removed, leaves torn in half lengthwise and cut into ½-inch strips
¼–½ teaspoon freshly grated nutmeg
¼ teaspoon sea salt, plus more to taste
2 pinches cayenne pepper

1. Preheat the oven to 350°F. Bake the sweet potatoes for about 1½ hours, or until they indent when poked with a finger. Remove from the oven (do not turn it off). Let them cool until you can handle them, about 10 minutes. To peel, pierce the skin with a knife and, gripping the skin between your thumb and the flat part of the knife blade, gently peel it back from the flesh, working around the potato, not down its length. Place the potatoes in a large bowl.

2. Meanwhile, heat the oil in a large skillet over medium-high heat. Add the collard greens and sauté, stirring very frequently, until they begin to wilt, turn a darker green, and become slightly tender to the bite, 1½ to 2 minutes. Remove from the heat and transfer the greens to another bowl to stop them from cooking further.

3. Whip the potatoes with an electric mixer, scraping down the sides of the bowl, until smooth and fluffy. Fold in the nutmeg, salt, and cayenne, then whip the potatoes again to evenly incorporate the spices. Season with more salt to taste. Fold in the collard greens. (This dish can be prepared in advance up to this point.)

4. Place in a 9-x-13-inch baking dish, cover with foil, and bake for 20 minutes, or until heated through. Serve immediately.

Nondairy Mashed Potatoes

Mashed potatoes are always a favorite, but they're usually laden with dairy products and fat. This recipe cuts the fat considerably and substitutes tofu for the dairy products. I have served these potatoes to crowds without initially disclosing their nondairy status — always to rave reviews and disbelief when the secret is finally revealed. The potatoes are superb with Garden Brown Sauce (page 200), Quinoa-Mushroom Nut Loaf (page 86), and Tahini Butternut Squash (page 105).

MAKES 6 TO 8 SERVINGS

1½ pounds soft tofu
4 pounds Idaho (russet) potatoes, peeled and cut into
    1½-inch cubes
1 tablespoon sea salt
    Freshly milled black pepper

1. Puree the tofu in a food processor or blender, scraping down the sides, until smooth and creamy. Set aside.

2. Place the potatoes in a large pot of cold water and bring to a boil. Reduce the heat to low, cover, and simmer until the potatoes can easily be pierced with a fork, about 10 minutes. Drain and place in a large bowl.

3. Add the tofu to the potatoes and beat with an electric mixer or mash with a potato masher to the desired consistency. Add the salt and the pepper to taste and beat or mash until thoroughly incorporated. Serve.

NOTE: The potatoes can be refrigerated in a 9-x-13-inch baking dish, covered with foil, and reheated in a 350°F oven for about 20 minutes.

NO WORK, NO FOOD

Much of the practice and ritual of Zen in America today comes from ancient stories that were written down centuries ago in China and Japan and passed down through the generations. One such story is called "No Work, No Food" and concerns an eighty-year-old Zen master who worked in the garden every day alongside his students. Concerned about his health, his students decided to hide his tools from him so he could relax and not work so hard. After that, the teacher stopped eating. Days passed. The students worried and returned his tools. The teacher resumed working and eating. His teaching that day was, No Work, No Food.

The work practice of Zen monks and students is as important today as it was then and is an integral part of daily life at the monastery. Everyone works at something. Everyone contributes. Everyone feels useful. And everyone eats. No job is ranked higher or is more glamorous than any other job. Cleaning toilets is as important as gardening or office work. This work practice is an opportunity to sharpen one's skills at zazen: Do the task in front of you, with full concentration and delight. Chop wood, carry water. Nothing else. Just that.

—Myochi

Roasted Butternut Squash

This is a simple, delectable dish. Upon tasting it, people can't believe that there isn't more to the recipe than this.

MAKES 6 TO 8 SERVINGS

2 medium butternut squash (3–3½ pounds total), peeled and cut into 2-inch cubes
2 teaspoons canola or corn oil
¼ teaspoon sea salt

Preheat the oven to 400°F. Toss all the ingredients together in a large bowl. Roast on a baking sheet for 45 to 55 minutes, stirring after 15 minutes, 30 minutes, 40 minutes, and 50 minutes of cooking time. The squash is done when it is tender and lightly browned. Serve.

"Sooner or later, whatever we have to receive comes to us. Whether it is good or bad, we have no way to run away from it. This is the universal arrangement."

— Eido Roshi

Tahini Butternut Squash

I adapted this quick, versatile method of preparing butternut squash from my friend and eclectic vegetarian cooking cohort Julie Padwick. Serve over rice or as a side dish, or incorporate it into an elegant dinner menu.

MAKES 6 TO 8 SERVINGS

1 tablespoon olive oil
1 medium onion, chopped
¾ teaspoon sea salt, plus more to taste
1 large butternut squash (2–2½ pounds), peeled and cut into ½-inch cubes
1 cup Basic Vegetable Stock (page 134) or water
1 tablespoon tahini
Freshly grated nutmeg

1. Heat the oil in a large skillet over medium-high heat. Add the onion and salt and sauté, stirring occasionally, until the onion is almost translucent, about 5 minutes.

2. Stir in the squash and stock or water, increase the heat to high, and bring to a boil. Reduce the heat to medium-low, cover, and simmer, stirring occasionally, until the squash is tender and can easily be pierced with a fork, about 20 minutes.

3. Gently stir in the tahini and nutmeg. Season with additional salt, if needed, and serve.

Orange-Ginger Spaghetti Squash

This spaghetti squash is easily prepared yet fancy enough to grace a dinner-party table. It's good with Sesame Tofu (page 76) or Tofu Sashimi Platter (page 72).

MAKES 8 TO 10 SERVINGS

1 spaghetti squash (about 4 pounds), halved vertically and seeded
2 large oranges, peeled, seeded, and diced, juice reserved
3 scallions, thinly sliced on the diagonal (see page 45)
1 3-inch piece ginger, peeled and grated
  Sea salt

1. Preheat the oven to 375°F. Bring 6 to 8 cups water to a boil in a medium saucepan.

2. Place the spaghetti squash cut side down in a baking dish. Pour ¾ to 1 inch of boiling water into the dish. Bake for 1 hour and 15 minutes, or until you can easily scrape out and separate the long strands with a fork. The strands should be soft but still a bit crunchy. If the squash is not quite done, return it to the oven and check it again after 10 to 15 minutes. Carefully scrape all of the spaghettilike strands into a large bowl.

3. Mix in the oranges and reserved juice, 2 tablespoons of the scallions, and the ginger. Add salt to taste and toss thoroughly. Garnish with the remaining scallions. Serve warm or at room temperature.

Honey-Lemon Glazed Turnips

Many of our guests say they have never enjoyed turnips as much as they do with this sweet-and-sour glaze. Serve with Quinoa-Mushroom Nut Loaf (page 86) and Nondairy Mashed Potatoes (page 102) with Garden Brown Sauce (page 200).

MAKES 4 TO 6 SERVINGS

1 pound turnips, peeled and cut into 1-inch cubes (about 3 cups)
2 tablespoons fresh lemon juice
1 tablespoon honey
1 teaspoon potato starch (see page 67) or 2 teaspoons cornstarch
1½ teaspoons canola or corn oil
1 1-inch piece ginger, peeled and grated
Sea salt and freshly milled black pepper

1. Steam the turnips until you can easily pierce them with a fork, about 8 minutes. Remove from the heat and set aside; reserve 2 tablespoons of the steaming liquid.

2. Whisk together the reserved steaming liquid, lemon juice, honey, and potato starch or cornstarch in a small bowl. Set aside.

3. Heat the oil in a large skillet over low heat. Add the ginger and sauté until fragrant, about 2 minutes. Add the turnips and toss until coated with the oil. Add the lemon mixture, increase the heat to high, and bring to a boil. Reduce the heat to medium and cook, stirring frequently, until heated through, about 3 minutes. Season with salt and pepper to taste. Serve immediately.

TASTE

THE THIRD BOWL IN FORMAL MEALS IS OFTEN FILLED WITH SALAD, BUT IT'S rarely boring lettuce with tomato wedges and sliced cucumbers. Instead, I often use grated carrots or finely grated cabbage as a foundation for my salads, or I add potatoes, raw grated beets or kohlrabi, thinly sliced fennel, julienned daikon, or turnips.

Constructing a great salad is often as simple as using food from a previous meal creatively. Leftover steamed zucchini and carrots are wonderful in a light vinaigrette. Cooked spaghetti chopped into bite-size pieces, tossed with grated carrots, walnuts, raisins, chunks of apple and/or pineapple, and served with Lemon-Sesame Dressing makes a unique side dish. Pasta, grains, fruit, nuts, and seeds all lend themselves to a potential salad masterpiece. And most of these ingredients can be used as either the base of the salad or a flavorful addition.

It's important to choose a compatible dressing. Very few dressings combine well with every salad. The ones in this chapter will be your allies if you use them discreetly in your adventuresome salads.

—Seppo

Spinach Salad with Oranges and Walnuts

The sharp bite of red onion nicely balances the natural sweetness of fresh oranges in this tasty salad. The ingredients are layered for a beautiful presentation.

MAKES 4 TO 6 SERVINGS

6 cups fresh spinach leaves, rinsed well
6 ounces white mushrooms, cut into ¼-inch-thick slices (about 3 cups)
10 thin slices red onion, halved
1½ cups walnuts, toasted (see page 6)
1 large or 2 small oranges, peeled, seeded, and cut into ½-inch cubes (about 1 cup)
1 ripe Hass avocado, thinly sliced

Spicy Blue Cheese Dressing (page 128)

Toss the spinach with 2 cups of the mushrooms in a large bowl. Sprinkle half of the red onion on top of the spinach, then the walnuts, oranges, avocado, the remaining 1 cup mushrooms, and the remaining onion. Serve with the dressing on the side.

Cinnamon-Raisin Carrot Salad

This is a nondairy, unsweetened version of the classic recipe, with a touch of cinnamon. It's great on a hot day or alongside a spicy dish.

MAKES 4 TO 6 SERVINGS

½ cup raisins
½ pound soft tofu
2 tablespoons extra-virgin olive oil
1 tablespoon canola or corn oil
½ teaspoon ground cinnamon
½ teaspoon fresh lemon juice
½ teaspoon sea salt
8 large carrots, grated

1. Bring 1½ cups water to a boil in a small saucepan. Remove from the heat, add the raisins, cover, and let stand for 30 minutes. Drain and set aside.

2. Meanwhile, puree the tofu, both oils, cinnamon, lemon juice, and salt in a food processor or blender, scraping down the sides, until smooth and creamy.

3. Toss together the carrots, tofu dressing, and raisins in a large bowl. Refrigerate or serve immediately.

THE BUILDING

The construction of Dai Bosatsu Zendo was a perfect
merging of East and West. A local American architect
who had a dream of building an Oriental structure was
contracted to build it. He and our abbot, Eido Roshi,
spent a month together in Japan researching the project.
In the end, they decided to pattern Dai Bosatsu Zendo
after Tofuku Ji in Kyoto, Japan's largest Rinzai Zen
monastery, whose zendo is a national treasure.

The road up to Dai Bosatsu Zendo holds no clue that
you are about to arrive at an architectural wonder. At the
top of a curve in the road near the monastery sits an open-
sided woodshed about the size of two barns. Piled under
the roof are rows of split wood, used to heat the
monastery. At one moment, you can barely make out the
monastery through the pine trees, and at the next it is
revealed in all its glory in front of you. The outside is
decidedly Asian, with sloping roofs, white exterior walls,
and dark brown trim.

Inside, Tasmanian oak floors gleam in the dimly lit hallways. On the second floor, the hallways end in the Dharma Hall, with bright light streaming through its windows,
a beacon of warmth and calm with a huge golden Buddha statue sitting on the altar in total complacency. Altars
with water, incense, and flowers at each entrance and in
each large room look as though they have been tended to
only a moment before. The serene hush deepens as you
near the zendo. A sense of reverent awe that began at the
base of the mountain completes itself in this inner sanc-
tum of beauty.

—Myochi

Sesame-Walnut Slaw

This crunchy cabbage slaw accented with an Asian-style dressing is a good side dish with any Asian meal, or it can provide a distinct contrast to a spicy dish, such as Almond Thai Curry (page 64).

MAKES 4 TO 6 SERVINGS

2 teaspoons rice vinegar
2 teaspoons tamari
1 teaspoon sesame oil
½ medium green cabbage head, very thinly shredded (see page 72)
1 cup chopped walnuts, toasted (see page 6)
1 large carrot, grated
2 tablespoons sesame seeds, toasted (see page 6)

Whisk together the vinegar, tamari, and sesame oil in a small bowl. Toss the cabbage with the walnuts, carrot, and sesame seeds in a large bowl. Add the dressing and toss until it is thoroughly distributed. Serve.

Red Potato Salad with Asparagus and Artichoke Hearts

I save this favorite summer salad for special occasions and the occasional informal meal at the monastery. If you omit the blue cheese, you can transform it into a fabulous vegan dish. To make a nice presentation, mound the potato salad in the center of a serving plate covered with a generous bed of fresh spinach or arugula. The flavor of this salad improves if it is allowed to "sit in itself" overnight. It can be prepared up to two days in advance and refrigerated; the flavor gets better the longer you wait. Toss the salad every few hours, or whenever you think of it, so the dressing has a chance to permeate all of the potatoes.

MAKES 10 TO 12 SERVINGS

3 pounds red potatoes (15 or 16 small or 8 or 9 large [3-inch] potatoes)
1 pound fresh asparagus, 1 inch trimmed off the base and, if the stalks are thicker than a pencil, peeled
4½ tablespoons cider vinegar
1 tablespoon Dijon mustard
1½ teaspoons honey
¾ teaspoon sea salt, plus more to taste
6 tablespoons extra-virgin olive oil
1 14-ounce can whole artichoke hearts, drained, each heart cut vertically into eighths
3 ounces blue cheese (about ¾ cup), or more to taste, crumbled (optional)
2 tablespoons chopped fresh dill
Freshly milled black pepper
Fresh arugula or spinach (optional)

1. Place the potatoes in a large pot with enough water to cover and bring to a boil. Reduce the heat to low, cover, and simmer until they can be pierced with a fork, 15 to 20 minutes for small potatoes or 25 to 30 minutes for larger ones. Drain and let cool for a few minutes. Cut the potatoes into bite-size pieces and place in a large bowl.

2. Steam the asparagus until tender but not soggy, just until a knife can pierce the thick part of the stalk, 8 to 12 minutes. Immediately remove from the steam and transfer to a cutting board to cool. Slice into 1-inch lengths and add to the potatoes.

3. Whisk together the vinegar, mustard, honey, and salt in a small bowl. Drizzle in the olive oil, whisking until well blended and creamy. Add the artichokes and dressing to the potatoes and toss lightly.

4. Add the blue cheese (if using), dill, and pepper to taste. Toss lightly, taste, and adjust the seasoning with more salt, pepper, and/or blue cheese to taste. Refrigerate until serving time. Serve on a bed of arugula or spinach, if desired.

VARIATION

No-Frills Red Potato Salad

Omit the asparagus, artichoke hearts, and blue cheese. The dill can be omitted, too, though I prefer to use it. Add ¼ medium red onion, diced, and 1 large celery rib, diced.

"There is no such thing as the essence of dharma or the essence of ultimate reality apart from here and now."

— Eido Roshi

Three monks were traveling together to pay their respects to a Zen master who lived on a mountaintop and had a reputation for being an outstanding teacher. As they walked up the path, they noticed a large lettuce leaf floating down a stream alongside. They were disappointed to see this and agreed that if the "great" master was willing to waste even one piece of lettuce, he couldn't possibly be a worthy teacher. As they turned back, they saw the old master running along the stream with a butterfly net to catch the leaf. They immediately changed their minds and proceeded up the mountain.

— From an ancient Chinese
Zen anecdote, translated
by Eido Roshi

Fresh Tofu and Greens Platter with Pickled Ginger and Scallions

This salad is easy to put together and makes a breathtaking presentation as well. The red leaf lettuce can be replaced with another variety, and arugula or bean sprouts can be substituted for the watercress.

MAKES 4 TO 8 SERVINGS

3 cups packed red leaf lettuce, torn into large
    bite-size pieces
2 cups packed watercress, torn into bite-size pieces
2 pounds soft tofu, preferably fresh (see page 72), cut
    into 1-inch cubes
½ cup pickled ginger, rinsed well and drained
4 ounces sprouts, such as alfalfa, radish, or sunflower
3 scallions, thinly sliced on the diagonal (see page 45)
  Fresh lemon slices, halved (optional)
  Citrus Tamari (page 199) or tamari
  Wasabi paste (see page 45) or powder (optional)

1. Arrange the lettuce on a large serving platter, with the deep red pieces around the edge of the platter. Mound 1 cup of the watercress in the center of the platter.

2. Scatter three-quarters of the tofu on the lettuce. Arrange ½ cup of the remaining watercress over the tofu.

3. Sprinkle the remaining one-quarter of the tofu cubes over the watercress, avoiding the center mound. Scatter the remaining ½ cup watercress over the second layer of tofu.

4. Distribute the ginger over the watercress, avoiding the center mound. Pull apart the sprouts slightly and arrange them neatly on the center mound of watercress. Sprinkle the scallions over the ginger.

5. Garnish the platter with the lemon slices, if using. Serve with the citrus tamari or tamari and wasabi paste (if using), or whisk some wasabi powder into the tamari, if desired. Serve.

NOTE: The platter can be made a few hours in advance, covered with plastic, and refrigerated.

Faux Chicken Salad

Poached tempeh is a delicious understudy for chicken in this classic dish. The salad is good served on a bed of greens or spread on whole-grain bread. The flavor will be even better if you let it sit for a couple of hours.

MAKES 4 TO 6 SERVINGS

1 pound tempeh, cut into ½-inch cubes
3 tablespoons plus ½ teaspoon fresh lemon juice
4 scallions, thinly sliced on the diagonal (see page 45)
2 large celery ribs, chopped
½–¾ cup mayonnaise
1 teaspoon Old Bay seasoning
  Fresh lemon juice
  Sea salt and freshly milled black pepper

1. Place the tempeh in a medium saucepan with 4 cups cold water and 3 tablespoons of the lemon juice. Bring to a boil, reduce the heat to low, cover, and simmer for 20 minutes, or until the tempeh is somewhat swelled. Drain and let cool.

2. Place the tempeh, scallions, celery, mayonnaise, and Old Bay seasoning in a bowl and gently mix together. Season to taste with salt and pepper and the remaining ½ teaspoon lemon juice. Refrigerate and serve cold.

Beet Raita with Dill, Lime, and Honey

Raitas are usually served with spicy dishes to cool the palate. This nontraditional version does that in a vibrantly colorful manner. I often accompany this raita with Japanese-Style Curry (page 66).

MAKES ABOUT 3 CUPS

¾ cup plain low-fat yogurt
2 tablespoons chopped fresh dill
1½ teaspoons honey
1½ teaspoons fresh lime juice
1 medium beet (about ½ pound), peeled and grated

Whisk together the yogurt, dill, honey, and lime juice in a medium bowl. Add the beet and mix thoroughly. Refrigerate and serve cold.

Cucumber-Grape Raita with Tofu

This nondairy raita uses pureed soft tofu as its base. Fresh and lively, it's the perfect accompaniment to Almond Thai Curry (page 64) or Japanese-Style Curry (page 66).

MAKES ABOUT 4 CUPS

1 pound soft tofu
5–7 tablespoons fresh lemon juice
1 tablespoon canola or corn oil
¾ teaspoon sea salt
4 Kirby (4-to-5-inch pickling-type) cucumbers, seeded and sliced
1 cup seedless green grapes
½ cup packed chopped fresh parsley

Puree the tofu in a food processor or blender with the lemon juice, oil, and salt, scraping down the sides, until smooth and creamy. Toss the dressing with the cucumbers, grapes, and parsley in a medium bowl. Refrigerate and serve cold.

DOKUSAN

During the weeklong silent retreat known as sesshin, each of us has an opportunity to meet twice a day with Roshi, the abbot, to discuss our meditation practice. This interview is called *dokusan*. As with so much else in the monastery, tradition surrounds the meeting. We all know when it's coming, since it's posted on the schedule that is meticulously followed. Nevertheless, the striking of the bell to announce dokusan can be startling, since no watches are allowed during sesshin.

We sit in the zendo in anticipation, waiting for Roshi's assistant monk, who sits in the adjoining Dharma Hall, to ring the bell. We don't know exactly when the moment will come. When the bell finally does ring — and not a moment before — all those who want to meet with Roshi jump up, grab their meditation cushions, and sprint to the Dharma Hall to get in line to see Roshi. First in, first served.

This rush to see the Zen master symbolizes our enthusiasm and our dedication to our practice and to solving our koan. Running can be risky, but it can also be quite invigorating: Rinzai Zen sport. After all the sitting, it is a refreshing contrast. Heart rates quicken. Concentration is at its peak, for if you are daydreaming, you will lose out. So many students want to see Roshi that not everyone can do so during each scheduled dokusan period.

The nearer you are to the altar in the zendo, the farther you have to run. Senior students have the advantage of experience in this competition, but the disadvantage of being closest to the altar. It levels the playing field, so to speak.

— Myochi

Sesame-Tamari Dressing

I often fall back on this easy dressing when I need one in a hurry. Nonetheless, it's always a hit with the crowd.

MAKES 1 CUP

¼ cup sesame oil
¼ cup rice vinegar
¼ cup tamari

Place all the ingredients in a jar with ¼ cup water and shake. Serve.

"Zazen is both something one does — sitting cross-legged, with proper posture and correct breathing — and something one essentially is. To emphasize one aspect at the expense of the other is to misunderstand this subtle and profound practice."

— Eido Roshi

Lemon-Sesame Dressing

A light sesame flavor and a subtle tang characterize this versatile dressing. It goes well with almost any food, including Asian dishes.

MAKES ABOUT 1 CUP

½ cup canola or corn oil
¼ cup cider vinegar
1 tablespoon plus 1 teaspoon fresh lemon juice
2 teaspoons sesame oil
2 teaspoons tamari
1 teaspoon Dijon mustard

Puree all the ingredients in a blender or food processor. (Alternatively, whisk together all the ingredients, except the oil, in a small bowl. Drizzle in the oil, whisking, until creamy and well blended.) Serve.

Ginger-Carrot Dressing

This is similar to the dressing that is typically served in Japanese restaurants in America, though it's much better. Serve over salad, rice, or vegetables.

MAKES ABOUT 1 CUP

½ medium onion, chopped
½ cup grated carrot
3 tablespoons fresh lemon juice
2 tablespoons mirin
2 tablespoons rice vinegar
1 tablespoon tamari
1½ teaspoons peeled and grated ginger
1 teaspoon sesame oil
½ teaspoon ground fennel seeds
1 tablespoon black sesame seeds (optional)

Puree all the ingredients, except the black sesame seeds, if using, in a blender or food processor. Fold in the sesame seeds. Serve.

Avocado-Wasabi Dressing

This is a luscious dressing with just a hint of wasabi flavor. It's sinfully good on any tossed green salad.

MAKES ABOUT 1¾ CUPS

2 ripe Hass avocados, peeled
1 tablespoon fresh lemon juice
2 teaspoons wasabi powder
1 teaspoon tamari
¼ teaspoon sea salt
½ cup chopped fresh cilantro (optional)

Puree all the ingredients, except the cilantro, if using, with ½ cup water in a blender or food processor, scraping down the sides, until smooth and creamy. Transfer to a small bowl and mix in the cilantro, if using. Serve.

"Just to be in the zendo is itself purification."

— Eido Roshi

THE MEAL CHANTS

If there is a large group of guests at a meal, *Namu Dai Bosa* is chanted over and over until everyone is served and the offering boards have been placed on the altar. *Namu Dai Bosa* means gratitude, and it is chanted often throughout the day. It's easy to learn. If everyone is familiar with the eating ritual, then we chant *Enmei Jukku Kannon Gyo* as we serve ourselves. This chant is a little more complicated and is usually the first long one that students memorize. Translated, it reads in part:

> *Salutation and devotion to Buddha!*
> *We are one with Buddha*
> *In cause and effect related to all Buddhas . . .*
> *Our True Nature is Eternal, Joyous, Selfless, and Pure . . .*

Once everyone is served and the signal is given, the names of the ten Buddhas are then invoked. During the chanting, unless we are serving ourselves, we rest our palms in prayer position in front of the heart. This gesture is called *gassho*, which means "palms together." Before we can eat, we chant *The Five Reflections*.

Then, in Japanese, we chant:

> *The first morsel is to destroy all evils*
> *The second morsel is to practice all good deeds*
> *The third morsel is to save all sentient beings*
> *May we all attain the path of Buddhahood.*

At the end of breakfast, we chant:

> *Having finished the morning meal, let us pray that all beings may accomplish whatever tasks they are engaged in and be fulfilled with all the Buddha dharmas.*

At the end of lunch, we chant:

Having finished the midday meal, our bodily strength is fully restored, our power extends over the ten quarters and through the three periods of time, and we are strong. As to the revolving wheel of dharma, no thought is wasted over it. May all beings attain true wisdom.

At both meals, we end with:

However innumerable all beings are
We vow to save them all
However inexhaustible delusions are
We vow to extinguish them all
However immeasurable dharma teachings are
We vow to master them all
However endless the Buddha's way is
We vow to follow it

All this, and eating, in just thirty minutes!

—Myochi

Spicy Blue Cheese Dressing

This dressing elicits praise and requests for the recipe whenever I serve it. It's best if made in advance and allowed to sit for a couple hours.

MAKES ABOUT 1¾ CUPS

6 ounces blue cheese, crumbled (about 1½ cups)
¾ cup mayonnaise
½ cup sour cream or plain low-fat yogurt
3 tablespoons fresh lemon juice
1 garlic clove, minced
1 teaspoon honey
1½–2 teaspoons red pepper flakes

Puree all the ingredients, except ½ cup of the blue cheese, in a food processor or blender, scraping down the sides, until smooth and creamy, about 30 seconds. Fold in the remaining ½ cup cheese and refrigerate for 2 hours before serving.

Lemon-Garlic Dressing

If you love garlic and lemon, this rich and creamy dressing is definitely for you. There are no subtle flavor intonations here. I serve it with strongly flavored greens, such as mustard, radicchio, or chicory.

MAKES ABOUT 1 CUP

3 garlic cloves, minced
¾ teaspoon sea salt
¼ cup fresh lemon juice
¼–½ teaspoon red pepper flakes (optional)
½ cup extra-virgin olive oil

Place the garlic and salt in a small bowl and mash with the back of a spoon until soft and creamy. Scrape the garlic mixture into a jar, add the lemon juice and red pepper flakes, if using, and shake well. Add the oil and shake until well blended. (Alternatively, you can whisk the dressing in a bowl.) Let sit for at least 30 minutes before serving.

"To sit, walk, and even trip and fall down are no other than the Perfect Way. To be silent, to laugh, and even to scream are the Perfect Way. Everyday action is the Perfect Way. If this is understood, there is no more worry about not being perfect."

—Eido Roshi

Honey-Dijon Dressing with Lime

This is my version of honey-mustard dressing. Those residents who are not usually salad fans always eat a lot when I toss the greens with this dressing.

MAKES ABOUT 1½ CUPS

½ cup canola or corn oil
½ cup Dijon mustard
⅓ cup honey
3 tablespoons fresh lime juice
2 pinches cayenne pepper

Place all the ingredients in a small bowl and whisk until creamy. Serve.

Strawberry-Cilantro Dressing

This dressing is light and fruity — a delightfully fresh way to top a plateful of mixed summer greens.

MAKES ABOUT 1½ CUPS

1 pint strawberries, hulled and halved or quartered (depending on size)
3 tablespoons rice vinegar
2 tablespoons fresh lemon juice
1 teaspoon vanilla extract
½ teaspoon maple syrup, plus more if needed
¼ teaspoon sea salt
¼ cup chopped fresh cilantro

Puree all the ingredients, except the cilantro, in a blender or food processor. Taste and season with additional maple syrup if the dressing is not sweet enough. Pour into a bowl and whisk in the cilantro. Serve.

Red Grape Dressing

Tiny pieces of grape skin add color and textural contrast to this light, slightly sweet dressing. Toss with vegetables and serve alongside a spicy dish to balance its bite.

MAKES ABOUT ¾ CUP

1 cup seedless red grapes
1 tablespoon plus 1 teaspoon canola or corn oil
1 teaspoon fresh lemon juice
1 teaspoon red wine vinegar
  Pinch sea salt

Place all the ingredients in a food processor or blender and blend until the grapes are liquefied. Serve.

"Chanting fills the gap between self and anxiety, self and worry, self and frustration, and self and various other negative thoughts, ideas, and phenomena."

— Eido Roshi

SOUP

SUPPER IS NOT TRADITIONALLY OFFERED IN JAPANESE ZEN BUDDHIST monasteries, so when it is served at Dai Bosatsu Zendo — generally only during the seven-day silent retreats of sesshin — it is conducted differently from other meals. There is no offering board passed down the table, and no incense is burned at the altars in the kitchen or dining room. The meal gong is not struck. Instead, a large set of wooden clappers call the diners to the table.

The center of the meal is always a big crock of piping hot soup. It can range from a simple broth with just a few vegetables floating in it, such as Ginger-Wakame Soup, to a hearty main dish, such as Cilantro-Lemon Vegetable Soup, to a refined puree, such as Butternut–Sweet Potato Soup. Freshly baked bread with a spread and a simple salad usually accompany the soup.

I try not to make too much soup at one time, since one of the main goals of the head cook is not to waste food. Nevertheless, because appetites wane during sesshin, there is often some left over, and after three or four meals we have enough different kinds to create a new soup. In monastery tradition, it is always called Melancholy Soup, though the results of the chance combinations are anything but. I'm often asked for the recipe, but each one is a once-in-a-lifetime creation.

Melancholy Soup, in fact, is a little like Zen teachings. We are given specific guidelines and instructions, yet we interpret them and carry them out in our own way. And, in each, the outcome is a surprise.

—Seppo

Basic Vegetable Stock

Making a good stock doesn't take much time or effort, just some planning. If you are preparing a complete meal, put the stock on before you do anything else and it will be ready in plenty of time. To give the stock added depth, I quickly roast the vegetables in the oven at a high temperature before boiling them.

On its own, this stock may not taste as you think it should, but its spirit will be revealed when other ingredients are added.

MAKES ABOUT 8 CUPS

2   medium onions, coarsely chopped
3   large celery ribs, cut into ½-inch-thick slices
3   large carrots, cut into ½-inch-thick slices
2   parsnips, peeled and cut into ½-inch-thick slices (optional)
2   zucchini, trimmed and cut into ½-inch-thick slices (optional)
1   whole garlic head, sliced horizontally
1   tablespoon olive oil
6   bay leaves

1. Preheat the oven to 450°F.

2. Place all the vegetables in a large pot. Add the oil and toss to coat. Place the vegetable mixture on a baking sheet and roast for 10 minutes. Stir and roast for 5 minutes more. Do not brown.

3. Transfer the vegetable mixture back to the pot and add 12 cups cold water and the bay leaves. Bring to a boil, reduce the heat to low, and simmer, uncovered, for 30 minutes. Let stand for 10 minutes. Pour through a strainer, discarding the solids, and use as directed.

NOTES: Many other vegetables can be added to the stock. I routinely save stems from fresh herbs and vegetable parings and skins. A small amount of nutritional yeast (about 1½ tablespoons for this recipe) can be added for a poultrylike flavor. If the vegetable isn't fresh, don't use it. Strongly flavored vegetables and those in the cabbage family, such as broccoli and collard greens, should be added in moderation unless you intend to use the stock for a broccoli or greens soup. I never add salt or tamari to a stock, reserving that for the soup or sauce recipe. Vegetable stock can safely be stored in the refrigerator for only 2 days. I immediately freeze any leftovers.

Quick Miso Soup

This is a great recipe to have on hand when you have unexpected guests or need to come up with a comforting hot soup quickly. It takes only a little more time than boiling water. It's also a nice way to start an Asian-style meal.

MAKES 4 TO 6 SERVINGS

½ cup plus 1 tablespoon white miso
1½ teaspoons tamari
¼ teaspoon sea salt
½ pound tofu (any kind), cut into ½-inch cubes
3 scallions, thinly sliced on the diagonal (see page 45)

1. Bring 8 cups cold water to a boil in a large saucepan. Remove from the heat. Ladle about 2 cups of the water into a bowl and thoroughly whisk in the miso. Return the miso mixture to the saucepan and stir in the tamari and salt.

2. Divide the tofu and scallions evenly among individual bowls. Ladle the soup into the bowls and serve immediately.

THE THIRD MEAL

The seven-day silent retreat of sesshin is the only time a third formal meal is served in the monastery. This supper falls outside tradition. Its purpose is to supply the participants with the energy to continue. Since sesshin can be physically grueling, with fourteen hours of each day spent sitting, kneeling, bowing, and chanting, this meal is a much-needed and welcome repast. By 5:00 P.M., we've all been awake for more than twelve hours, and we have another four hours of meditation ahead of us before the day's end.

But this third meal is special for reasons other than the relief and requisite fuel it brings. The unpredictability of what is served makes it memorable. Though we can be pretty sure that supper will include soup, bread, and salad, none of them is ordinary. The rich colors touch our heightened senses. The tastes explode in our mouths and bring an almost guilty pleasure.

The third meal reminds us once again of the truth of impermanence — whatever pain we were feeling recedes to the back of our minds as the food in front of us demands our full concentration. The fact that it has been lovingly and mindfully prepared does not escape our attention. Even without the chanting, we cannot help but feel gratitude for such a feast.

—Myochi

Mushroom-Daikon Miso Soup

Serve this rich, mellow, and easy-to-prepare soup as a light starter for any Asian-style meal or with rice and a simple vegetable dish or salad.

MAKES 4 TO 6 SERVINGS

12 ounces white mushrooms, cut into ¼-inch-thick slices
1 4-inch piece daikon, peeled, halved lengthwise, and cut into ¼-inch-thick slices
¼ cup plus 1 tablespoon white miso
2 tablespoons red miso
Scallions, thinly sliced on the diagonal (see page 45; optional)
1 teaspoon tamari

1. Place 8 cups cold water, the mushrooms, and daikon in a large saucepan. Bring to a boil, reduce the heat to low, cover, and simmer for 30 minutes.

2. Ladle about 1½ cups of the broth into a small bowl and thoroughly whisk in the white and red miso. Return the miso mixture to the saucepan. Stir in the scallions, if using, and the tamari. Serve immediately.

NOTE: For a heartier version, add ½ pound tofu, cut into ½-inch cubes, just before serving.

Mushroom-Barley Miso Soup

Don't let the usual light connotations of miso soup sway you — this soup is very hearty and perfect for a cold autumn or winter day. Serve with crackers or pita bread and Lentil-Walnut Pâté (page 190) for a simple meal. A food processor can help out with slicing the mushrooms.

MAKES 8 TO 10 SERVINGS

¾ cup barley, rinsed well and drained
¼ cup canola or corn oil
2 medium onions, chopped
¾ teaspoon sea salt, plus more to taste
1¼–1½ pounds white mushrooms, cut into ¼-inch-thick slices
5 garlic cloves, minced
3 tablespoons tamari, plus more to taste
⅓ cup white miso, plus more to taste

1. Place 2¼ cups water and the barley in a medium saucepan. Bring to a boil, reduce the heat to low, cover, and simmer until most of the water has been absorbed and the barley is tender, about 40 minutes.

2. Heat the oil in a large pot over medium-high heat. Add the onions and salt and sauté, stirring occasionally, until the onions begin to soften, about 2 minutes. Add the mushrooms and garlic and sauté until the mushrooms have exuded their juices and the onions are translucent, about 10 minutes more.

3. Add 7 cups cold water to the pot and bring to a boil. Reduce the heat to low, add the barley (making sure to scrape all the cooking liquid from the saucepan) and tamari, and simmer for 10 minutes.

4. Whisk together ½ cup hot (not boiling) water and the miso in a small bowl. Stir the miso mixture into the soup and season to taste with additional salt, tamari, or miso, if desired. Serve.

NOTE: Don't boil the soup once the miso has been added. Boiling miso not only alters its taste but also diminishes its nutritional benefits. Leftover soup should be reheated over moderate heat, taking care not to let it boil.

Ginger-Wakame Soup

This delicate soup is an appropriate way to start a lunch or a Japanese-style meal. The shape of the ginger and scallions is an intrinsic part of this soup's presentation. It's a superb complement to Sesame Tofu (page 76).

MAKES 6 TO 8 SERVINGS

⅓ ounce dried wakame (about 2 cups)
¼ cup plus 2 tablespoons tamari
1 3-inch piece ginger, peeled and cut into thin matchsticks (see below)
3 tablespoons sake
2 teaspoons mirin
½ teaspoon sea salt
½ pound tofu (any kind), cut into ¼-inch cubes (optional)
4 scallions, cut into ⅛-to-¼-inch pieces on the diagonal (see page 45)

1. Place the wakame and 8 cups cold water in a large bowl. Cover and let stand at room temperature for 1 hour. The wakame will absorb water and become tender, and the water will take on the subtle essence of the wakame.

2. Drain the wakame, making sure to reserve the broth, and cut into bite-size pieces. Set aside. Strain the wakame broth through a fine sieve or a coffee filter placed in a strainer set over a large saucepan to remove any dirt.

3. Place the wakame broth over high heat. Add the tamari, ginger, sake, mirin, and salt and bring to a boil. Let boil for 3 minutes, remove from the heat, and stir in the wakame, tofu (if using), and scallions. Serve immediately.

TO CUT GINGER INTO THIN MATCHSTICKS: Once the ginger is peeled (see page 22), slice it as thinly as possible along the length of the root. Slice the ginger again, cutting as thinly as possible along the length of the ginger. You should end up with long matchstick-size pieces. Stack them and slice through their centers, making shorter matchsticks.

DON'T WASTE TIME

On top of every mountain is a ubiquitous, underlying sound. Anyone who has been to a mountaintop has heard it. Although you can't identify it or say, "Listen, do you hear that?" It almost seems to move. It shimmers.

It's as if the birds, the rush of the water over rocks, the deer tramping through the forest, the wild turkeys on this mountain are nestled in a blanket of sound that can't be heard but is nonetheless there. It penetrates to the bone and quiets all but the sound of breathing. This loud silence offers us a quintessential opportunity to hear and appreciate our breath, our own singular life. And it helps us to understand the interconnectedness of everything, which includes us.

There are also man-made sounds unique to this mountaintop. We are called to attention many times throughout a typical day by gongs, bells, and wooden sticks. The message being, Wake up! Now is the time. This moment is the moment. Don't waste time, breath, energy. Conduct your business, your chores, your sitting with a brisk attitude. Be attentive.

At dawn, dusk, and late evening, the sound of a wooden mallet striking a thick wooden block echoes through the woods, announcing the time of day. On the block is written: "Matter of life and death is great. Time runs quickly; nothing remains; it waits for no man. You should not waste your time." The mallet slowly wears the wood away, splinter by splinter, year by year. Traditionally, when a hole is worn clear through, a party is thrown in celebration.

For a moment the sound of the mallet rises above all others, penetrating the silence, then flows into the woods on an echo and becomes absorbed into the tapestry of all sound. I wonder, as I listen to it, what must the wildlife make of it? I imagine that by now, after more than twenty years on this mountaintop, this sound is probably as familiar to the birds, deer, and other wildlife that inhabit these woods as it is to the Zen students who visit and live here. Along with the other sounds from the percussion instruments of the monastery, it contributes to the calming effect of the mountain on all forms of life, wild and otherwise. How else to explain a deer eating a banana right from the palm of my hand?

—Myochi

Al Dente Vegetable Soup

The vegetables in this delightful soup are cooked only briefly, in Japanese style. The ingredients, however, weigh in a bit more on the American side.

MAKES 6 TO 8 SERVINGS

2 small potatoes (about ½ pound total), peeled and cut into eighths
2 large carrots, cut into ¼-inch-thick diagonal slices
2 large celery ribs, cut into ¼-inch-thick diagonal slices
1 small onion, cut into eighths
4 garlic cloves, thinly sliced
1 1½-inch piece ginger, peeled and thinly sliced
1½ teaspoons tamari
1 teaspoon sea salt, plus more to taste
2 medium tomatoes, cored and sliced into eighths
1 broccoli stalk, florets cut into bite-size pieces, stalk peeled and cut into ¼-inch-thick diagonal slices
1 cup chopped (1½-inch pieces) green cabbage
½ cup chopped fresh parsley or other fresh herb
1½–2 teaspoons fresh lemon juice

1. Place 6 cups cold water, the potatoes, carrots, celery, onion, garlic, ginger, tamari, and salt in a medium pot. Bring to a boil, reduce the heat to low, cover, and simmer for 5 minutes.

2. Add the tomatoes, broccoli, cabbage, and parsley or other herb. Cover and simmer for about 5 minutes more, or until the potatoes can easily be pierced with a fork. Stir in the lemon juice and additional salt, if desired. Serve hot.

A monk asked Master Ingen, "I understand in ancient days whenever people would come to master Joshu, he would say, 'Have a cup of tea.' Because of that, I have been saying to people whenever they come to my temple, 'Please dine with me.' What do you think about my style of teaching?"

Master Ingen hit him and said, "Say more."

The monk bowed and said, "Thank you for your guidance."

As the monk was about to withdraw, Master Ingen said, "If your relationship is truly pure, you don't have to invite your guest for lunch. But if you have some impure intention, even the purest tea will become the poison for both host and guest."

—From *The Sayings of Master Ingen*,
translated by Eido Roshi

Butternut–Sweet Potato Soup

Here's a memorable way to begin a Thanksgiving feast or autumn dinner party. Butternut squash and sweet potato harmonize beautifully, and their natural flavors shine through with only a few complementary ingredients. Baking the squash and sweet potato brings out a natural sweetness that you can't get from boiling.

MAKES 6 TO 8 SERVINGS

1 large butternut squash (2–2½ pounds), halved lengthwise and seeded
1 large sweet potato (about 1 pound), pierced a few times with a fork
1 tablespoon sesame oil
1 medium onion, chopped
1¼ teaspoons sea salt
1 1-inch piece ginger, peeled and grated
½ cup fresh orange juice
2 tablespoons maple syrup
Freshly milled black pepper
Sour cream (optional)
Chopped fresh chives or parsley (optional)

1. Preheat the oven to 350°F. Bring 4 cups water to a boil in a medium saucepan.

2. Place the butternut squash cut side down in a baking dish. Pour about ½ inch boiling water into the pan. Bake for 1 to 1¼ hours, until it can easily be pierced with a fork. Reserve any leftover cooking liquid. Set aside to cool.

3. Meanwhile, bake the sweet potato directly on the oven rack alongside the squash for 45 to 60 minutes, or until it can easily be pierced with a fork. Set aside to cool. You can also bake it for longer (until the squash is done); its flavor will be even sweeter.

4. Use a large spoon to scrape the flesh out of the squash and into a large bowl. Pierce the skin of the sweet potato with a knife and, gripping the skin between your thumb and the flat part of the knife blade, gently peel it back from the flesh, working around the potato, not down its length.

5. Heat the sesame oil in a large pot over medium heat. Add the onion and salt and sauté, stirring occasionally, until the onion is almost translucent, about 8 minutes. Add the ginger and sauté, stirring constantly, until the onion is translucent, about 2 minutes more. Add enough water to the squash-cooking liquid to equal 4 cups. Add this liquid and the orange juice to the pot and remove from the heat.

6. Add the squash and sweet potato to the onion mixture and mix well. Puree in a blender or food processor until smooth and creamy, in batches if necessary. Return the puree to the pot and reheat over low heat, whisking occasionally. Stir in the maple syrup and pepper. Taste and adjust the seasonings. Divide the soup among individual bowls and garnish each bowl with a dollop of sour cream, if using, swirling it through the soup. Sprinkle with the chives or parsley, if desired. Serve.

Cilantro-Lemon Vegetable Soup

Cilantro and fresh lemon give this traditional tomato-based main-course soup an adventurous flavor.

MAKES 4 TO 6 SERVINGS

2 tablespoons canola or corn oil
1 medium onion, chopped
1 teaspoon sea salt, plus more to taste
4 garlic cloves, minced
2 large carrots, chopped
2 large celery ribs, chopped
5 cups Basic Vegetable Stock (page 134) or water
1 large potato, peeled and cut into ½-inch cubes
½ cup tomato paste, plus more to taste
1 cup frozen lima beans
¼ cup fresh or frozen corn kernels
¼ cup fresh or frozen peas
⅓ cup finely chopped fresh cilantro
2 tablespoons fresh lemon juice
   Freshly milled black pepper

1. Heat the oil in a large pot over medium-high heat. Add the onion and salt and sauté, stirring occasionally, until the onion begins to soften, about 2 minutes. Add the garlic and sauté until the onion is translucent, about 5 minutes more. Add the carrots and celery and sauté until brightly colored, about 5 minutes more.

2. Add the stock or water, potato, and ½ cup tomato paste and bring to a boil. Reduce the heat to low, cover, and simmer until the potato can be easily pierced with a fork, about 15 minutes.

3. Add the lima beans, corn, and peas and return to a boil over high heat. Reduce the heat to low, add the cilantro and 1 tablespoon of the lemon juice, and simmer for 5 minutes. Season to taste with the remaining 1 tablespoon lemon juice, pepper, and more salt and tomato paste, if desired. Serve.

For an even heartier soup, you can add pasta. Use a small variety, such as tubettini, orzo, alphabet, or elbows. Cook ¼ cup dried pasta separately, drain, and add to the soup with the cilantro and lemon juice. Make sure the pasta is precooked, or it will soak up all the broth in the soup.

"Zen is not a philosophy. It is a way of life."

— Eido Roshi

DOING ZAZEN

In doing zazen, it is important to sit still and breathe deeply and naturally. To accomplish this, an erect and stable posture is necessary. The options:

1. THE LOTUS POSITION (the ideal posture for zazen but one that is difficult for most Westerners): Buttocks on the edge of the round meditation cushion, legs crossed, knees on the square mat on which the meditation cushion sits, feet and ankles resting on opposite thighs. This position tilts the pelvis slightly forward and opens up the lower belly for deep breathing.

2. THE HALF-LOTUS POSITION: Same as above, but with only one foot up on the opposite thigh, the other resting on the mat.

3. THE BURMESE POSITION: Both legs and feet crossed in front, with both knees and feet on the mat.

In these three postures, the tripod formed by the two knees and the buttocks supports the weight of the body and creates a stable and comfortable position. The spine is erect; the head rests comfortably on relaxed neck and shoulders. Hands are clasped gently in the lap, usually with the back of the left resting in the palm of the right, thumbs gently touching to form a slight circle.

4. THE SEIZA POSITION: This is the posture one assumes during formal tea ceremonies, but it can also be used for meditation. It is often the easiest position for beginners. One sits on knees and shins with buttocks resting on a bench or on a cushion placed between the legs.

Sometimes people who are not yet flexible enough to sit on cushions or who are recovering from an injury sit on a chair. As long as the diaphragm, belly, and lungs are open, and as long as the spine is erect, one can do zazen.

—Myochi

Creamy Root Vegetable Soup with Oats

Even people who do not usually favor root vegetables love this simple soup. The oatmeal brings out an added dimension of sweetness. Serve with Cinnamon-Currant Bread (page 168) for a comforting meal on a cold, snowy day.

MAKES 6 TO 8 SERVINGS

½ cup old-fashioned rolled oats
½ teaspoon dried rosemary, crumbled
3 small parsnips, peeled and cut into ½-inch cubes
3 large carrots, peeled and cut into ½-inch cubes
2 medium turnips, peeled and cut into 1-inch cubes
½ medium rutabaga, peeled and cut into ½-inch cubes
2 teaspoons sea salt

1. Bring 1¼ cups water to a boil in a medium saucepan. Add the oats, reduce the heat to low, and simmer until tender and thickened, 15 to 20 minutes. Remove from the heat and cool. Puree in a food processor or blender with the rosemary until smooth and creamy, about 30 seconds. Set aside.

2. Place 4½ cups cold water, the parsnips, carrots, turnips, and rutabaga in a large pot and bring to a boil. Reduce the heat to low, cover, and simmer until the vegetables are tender but not mushy, about 20 minutes. Stir in the pureed oatmeal and salt. Serve.

Butternut–Black Bean Soup

Sweet butternut squash and black beans produce a one-of-a-kind autumn soup. Match it with Coconut Corn Bread (page 164) with Tahini-Applesauce Spread (page 201) and a salad.

MAKES 8 TO 10 SERVINGS

2 cups black beans, sorted, rinsed well, and drained
2 tablespoons canola or corn oil
1 medium onion, chopped
2 teaspoons sea salt
4 garlic cloves, minced
2 large butternut squash (2–2½ pounds each), peeled and cut into ¾-to-1-inch cubes (5–6 cups)
2 teaspoons tamari
Freshly milled black pepper
Sour cream (optional)
Chopped fresh cilantro (optional)

1. Place the beans in a pot with enough cold water to cover by a few inches and bring to a boil. Boil for 3 to 5 minutes. Remove from the heat, cover, and let stand for 1 hour. (Alternatively, if you have the time and the foresight, you can soak the beans at room temperature for at least 4 hours or overnight.) Rinse the beans thoroughly.

2. Heat the oil in a large pot over medium-high heat. Add the onion and salt and sauté, stirring occasionally, until the onion is almost translucent, about 5 minutes. Add the garlic and sauté until the onion is very soft, about 5 minutes more. Stir in 7 cups water, the squash, and beans and bring to a boil. Reduce the heat to low, cover, and simmer, stirring occasionally, until the beans are tender but not mushy, about 1 hour.

3. Remove 1 cup of the beans and vegetables and at least 1 cup of the broth and puree in a blender or food processor. Return the puree to the pot. (If you want a thicker soup, puree more of the beans and vegetables.) Add the tamari and pepper to taste and simmer for 5 minutes more. Divide the soup among individual bowls, garnish each with a dollop of sour cream and a sprinkling of cilantro, if desired. Serve.

Pinto Bean Soup

Pinto beans have so much character that few additions are needed to bring out their full flavor and succulent texture. Serve with a warm basket of Semolina Rolls (page 162), with Coconut Corn Bread (page 164), or over a bed of rice with Roasted Butternut Squash (page 104).

MAKES 8 TO 10 SERVINGS

4 cups pinto beans, sorted, rinsed well, and drained
2 tablespoons canola or corn oil
1 medium onion, chopped
1 tablespoon plus ½ teaspoon sea salt
6–8 garlic cloves, minced
6 bay leaves
1 tablespoon tamari
Freshly milled black pepper

1. Place the beans in a pot with enough cold water to cover by a few inches and bring to a boil. Boil for 3 to 5 minutes. Remove from the heat, cover, and let stand for 1 hour. (Alternatively, if you have the time and the foresight, you can soak the beans at room temperature for at least 4 hours or overnight.) Rinse the beans thoroughly.

2. Heat the oil in a large pot over medium-high heat. Add the onion and 1½ teaspoons of the salt and sauté, stirring occasionally, until the onion is almost translucent, about 5 minutes. Add the garlic and sauté until the onion is translucent, about 2 minutes more. Stir in 8 cups water, the beans, and bay leaves and bring to a boil. Reduce the heat to low, cover, and simmer, stirring occasionally, until the beans are tender but not mushy, about 1½ hours. Remove and discard the bay leaves.

3. Remove 1 cup of the beans and at least 1 cup of the broth and puree in a blender or food processor. Return the puree to the pot. (If you want a thicker soup, puree more of the beans.) Stir in the remaining 2 teaspoons salt, the tamari, and pepper to taste. Simmer for 5 minutes more. Serve.

BAKED GOODS

ENERGY

TWICE A MONTH, WE BAKE TWENTY TO THIRTY LOAVES OF YEAST BREAD IN the monastery. The aroma dances on wisps of air into the zendo, delighting our olfactory senses and challenging our focus. The bread is served for formal suppers and is very welcome. Some students have even been known to skip the rest of supper to indulge solely in bread.

When I'm caught between baking cycles and have no yeast bread on hand, I depend on quick breads. At other times, I'll whip some up for a change of pace and to have an impromptu fresh-out-of-the-oven treat. Honey-Graham Muffins and their variations have become particular favorites. Leftovers, which are rare, are great for snacking. Some, like Cinnamon-Currant Bread, can even be toasted or made into French toast.

Of the breads in this chapter, some, such as Lemon–Poppy Seed Bread, Pear-Cardamom Bread, and Morning Glory Muffins, are more suited for brunch or breakfast.

—Seppo

Corn-Oat Bread

This slightly sweet bread has a dense crumb and subtle whole-grain flavor. It's easy to make if the sponge is started the night before and you're planning to be around the house the next day, since it needs attention only at intermittent stages. There is one rule that you must remember: all rising must occur at 74° to 80°F.

MAKES 2 LOAVES

SPONGE
½ teaspoon active dry yeast
¾ cup whole wheat bread flour

CORN-OAT MIXTURE
¾ cup old-fashioned rolled oats
¾ cup coarse cornmeal
¼ cup honey
2 teaspoons sea salt

DOUGH
½ teaspoon active dry yeast
5½–6½ cups whole wheat bread flour

1. SPONGE: Sprinkle the yeast into ½ cup water in a small bowl. Do not disturb until it begins to dissolve, about 3 minutes. Stir until creamy and the yeast has completely dissolved.

2. Stir in the flour to make a thick batter, then stir about 100 strokes, or until the gluten has begun to form and the batter can be pressed off the spoon onto the side of the bowl. (This fully distributes all the ingredients, incorporates oxygen, and begins the formation of the gluten.)

3. Scrape down the sides of the bowl and cover with a clean, damp kitchen towel, an inverted bowl, or plastic wrap to keep the sponge moist. Let rise for 2 to 10 hours, or until the sponge is soft, aromatic, and full of bubbles.

4. CORN-OAT MIXTURE: Meanwhile, combine all the ingredients with 2 cups water in a medium saucepan. Bring to a low boil over medium heat, stirring occasionally; immediately remove from the heat. Let cool to room temperature, about 1 hour.

5. DOUGH: Sprinkle the yeast into ¼ cup water in a medium bowl. Do not disturb until it begins to dissolve, about 3 minutes. Stir until creamy and the yeast has completely dissolved.

6. Add the sponge and stir or mix with your hands until thoroughly combined.

7. Mix in 1 cup of the flour. Add the corn-oat mixture and 4 cups of the flour, 1 cup at a time, until a thick dough forms that is too stiff to stir with a spoon.

8. Transfer the dough to a lightly floured work surface and knead for 15 minutes, incorporating the remaining ½ to 1½ cups flour as you knead. If the dough is too dry, add water by moistening your hands as you work. If it is too moist, sprinkle a tablespoon of flour on the work surface and incorporate it as you knead. At the end, you should have dough that is smooth, pliable, somewhat pale, and not at all sticky. The dough is ready when it springs back after being poked with a finger. (Set a timer: 15 minutes can seem like a long time when kneading a whole-grain dough.)

9. Lightly coat a large bowl with spray, oil, or butter. Place the dough in the bowl; cover with a clean, damp kitchen towel, an inverted bowl, or plastic wrap. Let rise until doubled in volume, 2 to 3 hours. (An indentation should remain when you poke your finger ½ inch into the dough.)

10. Coat two 9-x-5-x-3-inch loaf pans with spray, oil, or butter and set aside.

11. Place the dough on a lightly floured work surface. Gently press flat to remove any trapped gas. Do not punch down the dough; it may damage the gluten net formed during kneading. Form the dough into a ball and cut into 2 equal pieces. Shape each piece into a long rectangle, about 18 inches long and 5 inches wide. To form a loaf, fold the ends over the top, overlapping them. Turn the dough over and smooth down the sides with your hands. Pinch the bottom and side seam together.

12. Place the shaped dough in the loaf pans, cover with a clean, damp kitchen towel, an inverted bowl, or plastic wrap, and let rise again until the volume has increased one and a half times, 1 to 1½ hours.

13. Meanwhile, after the bread has risen for about 30 minutes, preheat the oven to 450°F. (Remove the light bulb from your oven before preheating to avoid breakage when spritzing the bread with cold water during baking.)

14. Score the risen loaves with a sharp knife or razor blade by making several cuts ¼ to ½ inch deep along the surface at a 45° angle.

15. Place the loaves on the center rack of the oven. Quickly spray the inner walls and floor of

the oven with cold water from a spray bottle. (I use a plant mister.) Quickly shut the door to trap the steam and repeat this process twice more at 3-minute intervals. (This creates steam that will help form a thick, crunchy crust.)

16. Bake for 11 minutes more, or until the crusts have begun to brown nicely. Reduce the oven temperature to 400°F. (If your oven bakes unevenly, as most do, this is an ideal time to switch the positions of the loaves.)

17. Bake for 15 to 20 minutes more, or until the bottom of a loaf makes a hollow sound when struck and the sides feel firm when given a light squeeze. If the bread isn't quite done, remove the loaves from the pans and set them directly on the oven rack. Bake for 5 minutes more, or until done.

18. Cool the loaves on a rack for at least 30 minutes before slicing.

NOTES: It's convenient to prepare the corn-oat mixture at the same time you make the sponge.

This recipe yields a beautiful loaf of bread whether or not you spritz the oven with water, but spritzing will give you a professional-quality crust.

One day when the Chinese Zen master Rinzai and Fuké were attending a dinner at a patron's house, the Master asked, "A hair swallows up the gigantic ocean and a mustard seed contains Mount Sumeru. Is this a wondrous activity of supernatural power or the fundamental substance as it is?"

Fuké kicked over the dinner table. "How coarse!" cried the Master. "What place do you think this is, talking about coarse and fine?" said Fuké.

The following day, Master Rinzai and Fuké again attended a dinner. The Master asked, "How does today's feast compare with yesterday's?"

Fuké again kicked over the dinner table. "Good enough," said the Master, "but how coarse!"

"Blind fellow," said Fuké. "What's Buddha Dharma got to do with coarse and fine?"

The Master stuck out his tongue.

—From *Rinzairoku*,
translated by
Eido Roshi

Soy Milk Bread

Soy milk lends dairy-free richness to this tender, mild-flavored whole-grain bread. Tahini-Miso Sauce (page 201), Roasted Eggplant and Red Pepper Hummus (page 193), or any of the hummus variations goes wonderfully with this bread.

MAKES 2 LOAVES

SPONGE

½ teaspoon active dry yeast
¾ cup whole wheat bread flour

DOUGH

About 2½ cups soy milk
½ teaspoon active dry yeast
5½–6½ cups whole wheat bread flour
2 teaspoons sea salt

1. SPONGE: Sprinkle the yeast into ½ cup water in a small bowl. Do not disturb until it begins to dissolve, about 3 minutes. Stir until creamy and the yeast has completely dissolved.

2. Stir in the flour to make a thick batter, then stir about 100 strokes, or until the gluten has begun to form and the batter can be pressed off the spoon onto the side of the bowl. (This fully distributes all the ingredients, incorporates oxygen, and begins the formation of the gluten.)

3. Scrape down the sides of the bowl and cover with a clean, damp kitchen towel, an inverted bowl, or plastic wrap to keep the sponge moist. Let rise for 2 to 10 hours, or until the sponge is soft, aromatic, and full of bubbles.

4. DOUGH: Place the soy milk in a medium bowl and sprinkle with the yeast. Do not disturb until it begins to dissolve, about 3 minutes. Stir until creamy and the yeast has completely dissolved.

5. Add the sponge and stir or mix with your hands until thoroughly combined.

6. Mix in 1 cup of the flour. Add the salt and 4 cups of the flour, 1 cup at a time, until a thick dough forms that is too stiff to stir with a spoon.

7. Transfer the dough to a lightly floured work surface and knead for 15 minutes, incorporating the remaining ½ to 1½ cups flour as you knead. If the dough is too dry, add water or more soy milk by moistening your hands as you work. If it is too moist, sprinkle a tablespoon of flour on the work surface and incorporate it as you knead. At the end, you should have dough that is smooth, pliable, somewhat pale, and not at all sticky. The dough is ready when it springs back after being poked with a finger. (Set a timer: 15 minutes can seem like a long time when kneading a whole-grain dough.)

8. Lightly coat a large bowl with spray, oil or butter. Place the dough in the bowl; cover with a clean, damp kitchen towel, an inverted bowl, or plastic wrap. Let rise until doubled in volume, 2½ to 3 hours.

9. Deflate the dough by pushing down in the center and pulling up the sides. Do not punch down the dough; it may damage the gluten net formed during kneading. Turn out the dough onto the work surface, reshape it into a ball, and let stand, covered with the inverted bowl, for 30 minutes.

10. Coat two 8½-x-4½-inch loaf pans with spray, oil, or butter and set aside.

11. Gently press the dough flat. (There is no need to remove all the air pockets in the dough.) Form the dough into a ball and cut into 2 equal pieces. Shape each piece into a long rectangle, about 18 inches long and 5 inches wide. Fold the ends over the top, overlapping them. Turn the dough over and smooth down the sides with your hands. Pinch the bottom and side seams together.

12. Place the shaped dough in the loaf pans, cover with a clean, damp kitchen towel, an inverted bowl, or plastic wrap, and let rise until the volume has increased one and a half times, 1½ to 2 hours.

13. Meanwhile, after the bread has risen for about 30 minutes, preheat the oven to 450°F. (Remove the light bulb from your oven before preheating to avoid breakage when spritzing with cold water during baking.)

14. Score the risen loaves with a sharp knife or razor blade by making several cuts ¼ to ½ inch deep along the surface at a 45° angle.

15. Place the loaves on the center rack of the oven. Quickly spray the inner walls and floor of the oven with cold water from a spray bottle. (I use a plant mister.) Quickly shut the door to trap the steam and repeat this process twice more at 3-minute intervals. (This creates steam that will help form a thick, crunchy crust.)

16. Bake for 11 minutes more, or until the crusts have begun to brown nicely. Reduce the oven temperature to 400°F. (If your oven bakes unevenly, as most do, this is an ideal time to switch the positions of the loaves.)

17. Bake for 15 to 20 minutes more, or until the bottom of a loaf makes a hollow sound when struck and the sides feel firm when given a light squeeze. If the bread isn't quite done, remove the loaves from the plans and set them directly on the oven rack. Bake for 5 minutes more, or until done.

18. Cool the loaves on a rack for at least 30 minutes before slicing.

NOTE: All rising must occur in a moderately warm environment of 74° to 80°F.

THE DOKUSAN ROOM

Flickering candles, burning incense, soft light, and the Zen master's imposing presence all contribute to the awe and reverence we carry into the dokusan room, where we meet our teacher for private consultation about our meditation practice. Like all serious encounters in the monastery, the meeting takes place on the floor. There Roshi sits, regally garbed in his master's robes, cross-legged, waiting for our entrance, not moving until we are in our place opposite him. Face to face: students and master.

As with everything else at the monastery, the meeting reflects one of the basic tenets of Zen: unpredictability. Most times, Roshi speaks; sometimes he only rings his bell, indicating that the session is over. Generally, all he says is yes or no; mostly no. This is our practice, not his. He is only a guide. We are given no answers, and yet they are offered to us. By the clock, this encounter lasts but a few minutes. Sometimes cosmic shifts take place. At other times, only minute understanding dawns. Or confusion. Any of these responses may spark renewed determination. In any case, it is time well spent.

—Myochi

Semolina Rolls

These soft dinner rolls are versatile enough to be served with any main course or soup. The dough can also be shaped into sandwich rolls or long, thin loaves. (One batch works beautifully for an 18-inch Sicilian pizza crust.) My friend Suzanne Geffre initially developed this recipe, and I altered it a bit to suit our needs at Dai Bosatsu.

MAKES SIXTEEN 3-INCH ROLLS
OR TWO THIN 18-INCH LOAVES

2 tablespoons honey
1 tablespoon active dry yeast
2 tablespoons olive oil
1¾ cups whole wheat bread flour
1½ cups semolina flour
2 tablespoons dry milk
1½ teaspoons sea salt
   Coarse cornmeal (optional)
1 large egg white (optional)

1. Whisk 1¼ cups warm water (75° to 85°F) and the honey in a small bowl. Sprinkle in the yeast and do not disturb until it begins to dissolve, about 3 minutes. Add the olive oil and stir until creamy and the yeast has completely dissolved.

2. Combine the whole wheat flour, semolina flour, dry milk, and salt in a large bowl and make a well in the center. Add the yeast mixture and stir until thoroughly combined.

3. Transfer the dough to a lightly floured work surface and knead for about 10 minutes. If the dough is too dry, add water by moistening your hands as you work. If it is too moist, sprinkle the work surface with a tablespoon of flour and incorporate it as you knead. During the kneading, the dough will feel a bit tacky, but not actually sticky. At the end, you should have dough that is smooth and not at all sticky.

4. Lightly coat a large bowl with spray, oil, or butter. Place the dough in the bowl; cover with a clean, damp kitchen towel, an inverted bowl, or plastic wrap. Let rise until doubled in volume, about 45 minutes.

5. Dust a baking sheet with the cornmeal, if using. (If not using cornmeal, there is no need to grease the baking sheet.) To shape the dough into rolls, divide it into 2 equal pieces, then divide each of those into 2 pieces. Repeat twice more until you have 16 equal pieces of dough. Shape each piece into a round. Gently stretch the top of each roll down and under to the bottom. Place the rolls on the baking sheet. Or shape the dough into two 18-inch-long loaves and place on the baking sheet. Cover with a clean, damp towel and let rise until doubled in volume, about 1 hour.

6. Preheat the oven to 350°F.

7. Whisk the egg white, if using, with 1 tablespoon cold water. Before placing the bread in the oven, brush the rolls or loaves with the egg wash. Bake for 20 to 25 minutes for rolls, about 45 minutes for loaves, or until the tops are golden brown and the bottoms are a darker shade. Cool on racks. Serve.

Coconut Corn Bread

This moist corn bread is an all-time favorite. For a hearty meal, serve with Pinto Bean Soup (page 151) or Butternut–Black Bean Soup (page 150). Toast the corn bread and serve with maple syrup for breakfast, or enjoy it as a snack. If there is any left over, it won't last long.

MAKES ONE 9-X-5-INCH LOAF

DRY INGREDIENTS

1¾ cups coarse cornmeal
¾ cup whole wheat pastry flour or unbleached white flour
¾ cup shredded unsweetened coconut, toasted (see page 6)
1½ teaspoons baking soda
½ teaspoon baking powder
½ teaspoon sea salt

WET INGREDIENTS

1¾ cups plain low-fat yogurt
2 large eggs
¼ cup milk, soy milk, or rice milk
3–4 tablespoons maple syrup
2 tablespoons olive oil

1. Preheat the oven to 350°F. Coat a 9-x-5-x-3-inch loaf pan with spray, oil, or butter and set aside.

2. Combine all the dry ingredients thoroughly in a large bowl.

3. Whisk together all the wet ingredients in a medium bowl.

4. Add the wet ingredients to the dry and mix just until evenly blended, using as few strokes as possible.

5. Pour the batter into the loaf pan and spread evenly. Bake for 50 to 55 minutes, or until the bread is golden brown and a toothpick inserted in the center comes out clean. Cool on a rack for 10 minutes before slicing.

Coconut Corn Muffins

Divide the batter among sixteen 2¾-inch muffin cups coated with spray, oil, or butter. Bake for 25 to 35 minutes, or until the tops begin to brown.

NOTE: For best results, all the ingredients should be at room temperature. When mixing the wet and dry ingredients together, use as few strokes as possible. The more you mix the batter, the tougher the corn bread will be. However, the ingredients must be thoroughly combined, without lumps.

"The tenzo's cooking is artwork. It is crucial, as in other fine arts, to have a sincere and reverential attitude toward the ingredients, whether they are fine or coarse."

— From *Instructions for the Tenzo* by Zen Master Dogen, translated by Eido Roshi

Pear-Cardamom Bread

Moist, slightly sweet, and full of fresh pears, this delicious bread is robust with the flavor of cardamom. Depending on how sweet or spicy you want the bread to be, you can vary the amount of maple syrup and cardamom without adjusting the other ingredients.

MAKES ONE 9-X-5-INCH LOAF

DRY INGREDIENTS

- 2 cups whole wheat pastry flour or unbleached white flour
- ½ cup chopped walnuts or pecans, toasted (see page 6)
- 1 teaspoon baking soda
- ½–1 teaspoon ground cardamom
- ½ teaspoon ground cinnamon
- ½ teaspoon sea salt

WET INGREDIENTS

- ½ cup unsweetened applesauce
- 5–8 tablespoons maple syrup
- ¼ cup plain low-fat yogurt
- 2 large eggs
- 1 teaspoon vanilla extract

- 1 Anjou or Bosc pear, cut into ¼-inch cubes (1–1½ cups)

1. Preheat the oven to 350°F. Coat a 9-x-5-x-3-inch loaf pan with spray, oil, or butter and set aside.

2. Combine all the dry ingredients thoroughly in a large bowl.

3. Whisk together all the wet ingredients in a medium bowl.

4. Add the wet ingredients to the dry and mix just until evenly blended, using as few strokes as possible. Gently fold in the pear.

5. Pour the batter into the loaf pan and spread evenly. Bake for 50 minutes, or until the bread is toasty brown and a toothpick inserted in the center comes out clean. Cool on a rack for 10 minutes before slicing.

Pecan–
Sweet Potato
Spice Bread

The scent of this bread wafting through the house is perfect for the holidays — ginger and spice on a background of molasses. This bread is also great for brunch or afternoon tea, and it's an excellent use for leftover sweet potato. Cream cheese makes a very nice spread.

MAKES ONE 9-X-5-INCH LOAF

DRY INGREDIENTS

  2 cups whole wheat pastry flour or whole wheat flour
  1 cup chopped pecans or walnuts, toasted (see page 6)
  1 tablespoon baking powder
1½ teaspoons ground ginger
  1 teaspoon freshly grated nutmeg
  ½ teaspoon ground cinnamon
  ¼ teaspoon ground cloves
  ¼ teaspoon ground mace (optional)
  ¼ teaspoon sea salt

WET INGREDIENTS

  1 cup unsweetened applesauce
  ⅔ cup mashed cooked sweet potato (see below)
  ¼ cup plus 2 tablespoons molasses
  2 large eggs

1. Preheat the oven to 350°F. Coat a 9-x-5-x-3-inch loaf pan with spray, oil, or butter and set aside.

2. Combine all the dry ingredients thoroughly in a large bowl.

3. Whisk together all the wet ingredients in a medium bowl.

4. Add the wet ingredients to the dry and mix just until evenly blended, using as few strokes as possible.

5. Pour the batter into the loaf pan and spread evenly. Bake for about 1 hour, or until the bread begins to turn darker brown around the edges and a toothpick inserted in the center comes out clean. Cool on a rack for 10 minutes before slicing.

NOTE: To prepare sweet potato, peel, chop, and boil it for about 15 minutes, or until it is tender. Drain.

Cinnamon-Currant Bread

This is a hearty and nutritious bread that somehow maintains its lightness. Slightly sweet, it's great as a snack or with a bowl of hot soup. Serve with Tahini-Applesauce Spread (page 201) for the ultimate taste combination.

MAKES ONE 9-X-5-INCH LOAF

DRY INGREDIENTS

- 2 cups whole wheat pastry flour (or a combination of whole wheat pastry flour and graham flour, using up to 1 cup graham flour; see opposite page)
- ¾ cup wheat germ, toasted (see page 6)
- ½ cup dried currants
- 2½ teaspoons baking powder
- 2 teaspoons ground cinnamon
- ½ teaspoon baking soda
- ½ teaspoon sea salt

WET INGREDIENTS

- 1½ cups milk, soy milk, or rice milk
- ¼ cup canola or corn oil
- ¼ cup maple syrup
- 2 large eggs

1. Preheat the oven to 350°F. Coat a 9-x-5-x-3-inch loaf pan with spray, oil, or butter and set aside.

2. Combine all the dry ingredients thoroughly in a large bowl.

3. Whisk together all the wet ingredients in a medium bowl.

4. Add the wet ingredients to the dry and mix just until evenly blended, using as few strokes as possible.

5. Pour the batter into the loaf pan and spread evenly. Bake for 50 minutes, or until the bread is toasty brown and a toothpick inserted in the center comes out clean. Cool on a rack for 10 minutes before slicing.

NOTE: Regular whole wheat flour or unbleached white flour may be substituted in equal amounts for the pastry and/or graham flour.

Cinnamon-Currant Muffins

Divide the butter among twelve 2¾-inch muffin cups coated with spray, oil, or butter. Bake for 25 to 30 minutes, or until the edges begin to brown.

"Zazen practice is the practice of becoming. The practice of becoming when we are in trouble is to become the trouble itself. When you become a teacher, do what teachers do! When you become a student, do what students do! When you do zazen, do zazen and nothing else!"

— Eido Roshi

Lemon–Poppy Seed Muffins

These muffins are so full of lemony flavor that the thought of spreading anything on them will never cross your mind. Serve for breakfast or brunch.

MAKES TWELVE 2¾-INCH MUFFINS

DRY INGREDIENTS

- 2 cups whole wheat pastry flour or unbleached white flour
- 3 tablespoons poppy seeds
- 2½ teaspoons baking powder
- ½ teaspoon baking soda
- ¼ teaspoon sea salt

WET INGREDIENTS

- 1 cup unsweetened applesauce
- ½ cup honey
- ¼ cup canola or corn oil
- ¼ cup milk, soy milk, or rice milk
- 2 large eggs
- 1 tablespoon grated lemon zest
- Generous ¼ teaspoon lemon oil

1. Preheat the oven to 350°F. Coat a muffin tin with spray, oil, or butter and set aside.

2. Combine all the dry ingredients thoroughly in a large bowl.

3. Whisk together all the wet ingredients in a medium bowl.

4. Add the wet ingredients to the dry and mix just until evenly blended, using as few strokes as possible.

5. Fill each muffin cup with batter. Bake for about 25 minutes, or until the edges begin to brown. Remove from the pan and place on a cooling rack. Cool slightly and serve.

Lemon–Poppy Seed Tea Bread

Bake in a 9-x-5-x-3-inch loaf pan coated with
spray, oil, or butter for about 40 minutes, or until
a toothpick inserted in the center comes out
clean. Let cool for 10 minutes before removing it
from the pan. Cool completely on a wire rack
before slicing.

"The moment that we have or perceive any purposes or
objectives is the moment they become delusions."

—Eido Roshi

Honey-Graham Muffins

These muffins have the comforting flavor of graham crackers, with just a hint of cinnamon and ginger.

MAKES TWELVE 2¾-INCH MUFFINS

DRY INGREDIENTS

1½ cups graham flour
¾ cup wheat germ, toasted (see page 6)
1½ teaspoons baking soda
½ teaspoon baking powder
¼ teaspoon sea salt
⅛ teaspoon ground cinnamon
⅛ teaspoon ground ginger

WET INGREDIENTS

1 cup plus 3 tablespoons low-fat buttermilk
¼ cup canola or corn oil
1 large egg
2 tablespoons plus 1 teaspoon honey
2 teaspoons maple syrup
1 teaspoon molasses
1 teaspoon vanilla extract

1. Preheat the oven to 350°F. Coat a muffin tin with spray, oil, or butter and set aside.

2. Combine all the dry ingredients thoroughly in a large bowl.

3. Whisk together all the wet ingredients in a medium bowl.

4. Add the wet ingredients to the dry and mix just until evenly blended, using as few strokes as possible.

5. Fill each muffin cup with batter. Bake for about 20 minutes, or until the tops begin to brown. Remove from the pan and place on a cooling rack. For optimal taste, let cool completely before serving.

Multigrain Muffins

Substitute whole wheat pastry flour or regular whole wheat flour for the graham flour. Increase the ground ginger to ¼ teaspoon and omit the cinnamon. Add ½ cup old-fashioned rolled oats to the wet ingredients. Increase the buttermilk to 1¼ cups and omit the maple syrup and vanilla. Mix as instructed and bake for about 20 minutes, or until the tops begin to brown.

Orange–Raisin Bran Muffins

Substitute whole wheat pastry flour or unbleached white flour for the graham flour. Substitute ¾ cup bran for the wheat germ, omit the cinnamon and ginger, and add ½ cup raisins to the dry ingredients. Add 1 tablespoon grated orange zest and 1 teaspoon orange extract to the wet ingredients. Decrease the honey to 2 tablespoons, increase the molasses to 2 teaspoons, and omit the maple syrup and vanilla. Mix as instructed and bake for about 20 minutes, or until the muffins are golden.

Morning Glory Muffins

These robust breakfast muffins are hearty, yet moist and light.

MAKES TWELVE 2¾-INCH MUFFINS

DRY INGREDIENTS

- 2 cups whole wheat pastry flour or whole wheat flour
- 2½ teaspoons baking soda
- 1 teaspoon ground ginger
- 1 teaspoon ground cinnamon
- ½ teaspoon sea salt

- 2 cups grated carrots
- 1 cup peeled and grated apple
- ½ cup raisins
- ½ cup chopped almonds, pecans, or walnuts, toasted (see page 6)
- ½ cup shredded unsweetened coconut, toasted (see page 6)

WET INGREDIENTS

- 3 large eggs
- ½ cup unsweetened applesauce
- ¼ cup plus 2 tablespoons honey
- 2 teaspoons molasses
- 1 teaspoon almond extract

1. Preheat the oven to 400°F. Coat a muffin pan with spray, oil, or butter and set aside.

2. Combine all the dry ingredients thoroughly in a large bowl. Add the carrots, apple, raisins, nuts, and coconut and mix well.

3. Whisk together all the wet ingredients in a medium bowl.

4. Add the wet ingredients to the dry and mix just until evenly blended, using as few strokes as possible.

5. Fill each muffin cup with batter, heaping it, since the muffins will not rise much. Bake for 15 to 20 minutes, or until the tops begin to brown. Remove from the pan and place on a cooling rack. Cool slightly and serve.

NOTE: To make muffins quickly in the morning, make the batter the night before and place it in the coated muffin cups. Wrap the entire pan in plastic and refrigerate overnight. In the morning, preheat the oven and place the muffins directly from the refrigerator into the oven. Bake for 20 to 25 minutes, or until the tops begin to brown.

Rosemary-Parmesan Dinner Muffins

I originally created these muffins to serve with pasta and marinara sauce when there was no time to make yeast bread. Serve with Pasta Puttanesca (page 58) or pasta with Classic Marinara Sauce (page 60). These muffins are also great as a snack and go well with most soups.

MAKES TWELVE 2¾-INCH MUFFINS

DRY INGREDIENTS

1½ cups unbleached white flour
½ cup whole wheat pastry flour or whole wheat flour
½ cup freshly grated Parmesan cheese
¼ cup coarse cornmeal
1 tablespoon baking powder
2 teaspoons dried rosemary, crumbled
½ teaspoon sea salt

WET INGREDIENTS

1 cup milk, soy milk, or rice milk
¼ cup plus 1 tablespoon olive oil
2 large eggs

1. Preheat the oven to 350°F. Coat a muffin tin with spray, oil, or butter and set aside.

2. Combine all the dry ingredients thoroughly in a large bowl.

3. Whisk together all the wet ingredients in a medium bowl.

4. Add the wet ingredients to the dry and mix just until evenly blended, using as few strokes as possible.

5. Fill each muffin cup about two-thirds full of batter. Bake for 25 to 30 minutes, or until the tops begin to brown. Remove from the pan and serve immediately.

GASSHO

I often tell first-time visitors to the monastery who are overwhelmed by all the ritual that "when in doubt, gassho." Literally, *gassho* means "palms together." This gesture, with hands in prayer position in front of the heart, is used throughout the day and in many situations. Bowing at the entrance to the zendo, greeting others, chanting, and immediately before filling our bowls at meals are just a few of the gassho occasions.

By placing our hands in gassho, we immediately shift our point of view. The gesture inspires both reverence and gratitude. But like anything else, it can become an automatic response without meaning, so it is important to generate mindfulness even in this most simple act.

As Eido Roshi says, "One kind of gassho is just putting your hands together in a sort of absent-minded way. But there is another gassho when you truly put your palms together, without separating your fingers. Not only do you feel good when you gassho in this manner, but if someone happens to look at you, he can get inspiration from your sincere gassho." Gassho is a sweet tradition, easy to learn, and one that adds an exotic dimension to quotidian activities.

—Myochi

Irish Soda Bread

We love this bread. I adapted it from my mother's recipe, a tattered piece of paper that was cut from a women's magazine many years ago. The bread is not very sweet, nor is it high in fat, but it is full of flavor. Serve with breakfast or brunch, as a snack with tea or coffee, or as a light dessert. If two loaves sounds like too much, don't worry. You'll be grateful to have that second loaf to cut into.

MAKES 2 LOAVES

DRY INGREDIENTS

2¼ cups unbleached white flour
2 cups whole wheat pastry flour
1 tablespoon baking powder
2 teaspoons caraway seeds
1 teaspoon baking soda
1 teaspoon sea salt

1 cup raisins
4 tablespoons (½ stick) butter, chilled and cut into
    6–8 pieces

WET INGREDIENTS

1¾ cups low-fat buttermilk
1 large egg
3 tablespoons honey
2 tablespoons grated lemon zest

2 tablespoons whole wheat pastry flour, for sprinkling

1. Preheat the oven to 375°F. Coat two pie plates with spray, oil, or butter and set aside.

2. Combine all the dry ingredients thoroughly in a large bowl. Add the raisins and butter and cut in with a pastry blender or two knives until the mixture forms pea-size crumbs.

3. Whisk together all the wet ingredients thoroughly in a medium bowl.

4. Add the wet ingredients to the dry and mix just until evenly blended. Turn out onto a work surface floured with the 2 tablespoons whole wheat pastry flour. Knead until smooth, 2 to 3 minutes, incorporating the flour.

5. Divide the dough in half and shape each half into a round loaf. Place each loaf in a pie plate and press the dough to the sides of the plate. With a floured knife, cut 1-inch-deep crosses on top of the loaves. Bake until golden brown, about 35 minutes. For optimal flavor, let cool completely before serving.

"Let us cultivate our minds and make use of our minds,
instead of being used by our minds."

— Eido Roshi

Ginger-Butternut Biscuits

A daring twist on a classic idea, these biscuits are great any time but are especially delectable with Pinto Bean Soup (page 151) or Spicy Rice Bake with Black-Eyed Peas, Collard Greens, and Sweet Potato (page 36).

MAKES ABOUT 20 BISCUITS

2½ cups whole wheat pastry flour or unbleached white flour
1½ teaspoons sea salt
½ teaspoon baking soda
8 tablespoons (1 stick) unsalted butter, chilled and cut into ¼-inch cubes
1 small butternut squash (1–1½ pounds), peeled and cut into ½-to-1-inch cubes
¼ cup low-fat buttermilk
1 tablespoon peeled and grated ginger
2 teaspoons maple syrup

1. Combine the flour, 1 teaspoon of the salt, and the baking soda in a large bowl. Add the butter and cut in with a pastry blender or two knives until the mixture forms pea-size crumbs. Place the bowl in the refrigerator until the butter is hard, 15 to 20 minutes.

2. Meanwhile, preheat the oven to 450°F. Place the butternut squash in a medium saucepan with just enough water to cover. Add the remaining ½ teaspoon salt and bring to a boil. Reduce the heat to low and cook at a low boil until soft and not grainy, 10 to 15 minutes. Drain the squash (reserving the cooking liquid for soup stock, if desired) and puree it in a blender or food processor until smooth, about 30 seconds.

3. Whisk 1 cup squash puree, the buttermilk, ginger, and maple syrup in a medium bowl. Add to the flour mixture and stir until the dough comes together.

4. Turn the dough out onto a well-floured work surface (keep the surface well floured while kneading the dough). Knead 20 to 30 times, or until smooth, incorporating enough flour so the dough isn't sticky.

5. Pat the dough out until it is ½ inch thick. Cut into 2-inch rounds. Gather any scraps of dough, gently pat them together, and cut again. Place the rounds on an ungreased baking sheet. Bake for 13 to 15 minutes, or until the sides of some of the biscuits begin to split and the bottoms are quite brown. Do not let the bottoms burn. Remove from the oven and immediately place on a cooling rack. Cool slightly and serve.

FRAGRANCE

A SIMPLE TOPPING CAN CAST MAGIC ON A SLICE OF BREAD. INSTEAD OF delicately spreading the pâté, many of the residents have been known to heap it on their bread or even into their bowls. These toppings are as easy as they are tasty. They can be made in just the time it takes to puree several ingredients in a food processor.

Because of their simplicity, I often find myself inventing new spreads during zazen. Occasionally, a combination of ingredients will make my eyes pop open, as I realize the potential for a new recipe and try to "save" the idea for later recall.

Most of the eye-opening spreads and sauces in this chapter are versatile. They make wonderful appetizers on crackers or slices of baguette. Others can be tossed with vegetables, pasta, or grains, added to stir-fries, or used as the base of a salad dressing.

—Seppo

Portobello Pâté or Pastries

Portobello mushrooms make a savory filling for bite-size phyllo cups. If I have no frozen phyllo pastries on hand, I serve the mushroom filling as a pâté with a basket of crackers or a warm, crusty baguette. We often offer these pastries as an appetizer for celebration dinners. The filling can be made up to two days in advance and spooned into the cups just before serving. Count on five to eight pastries per person.

MAKES 2 CUPS PÂTÉ OR 45 PASTRIES

4 tablespoons (½ stick) unsalted butter
½ medium onion, diced
½ teaspoon sea salt, plus more for seasoning
1 garlic clove, minced
1 pound portobello mushrooms (about 3 medium), cut into ¾-inch cubes (see note)
½ cup dry white wine
Freshly milled black pepper
3 2.1-ounce boxes mini phyllo cups, thawed, or 1 baguette, warmed in the oven
1 red bell pepper, roasted (see opposite page), cut into thin 1½-inch-long slices, or paprika (optional)

1. Melt 2 tablespoons of the butter in a large skillet over medium heat. Add the onion and salt and sauté, stirring occasionally, until the onion is almost translucent, about 5 minutes. Add the garlic and sauté, stirring constantly, until the onion is translucent, about 2 minutes more. If the garlic starts to brown, reduce the heat.

2. Add the remaining 2 tablespoons butter to the skillet. When the butter is melted, add the mushrooms and sauté, stirring occasionally, until tender and beginning to soften around the edges, about 4 minutes. Stir in the wine and continue to cook until the liquid has evaporated, about 15 minutes. Season to taste with salt and pepper. Remove from the heat and set aside to cool.

3. Puree the mushroom mixture in a food processor, scraping down the sides as necessary. The pâté can be prepared up to this point and refrigerated.

4. If you are using the phyllo cups, remove the pâté from the refrigerator about 1 hour before filling the cups. Preheat the oven to 350°F. Using a spoon, fill each cup with about 2 teaspoons mushroom mixture. Place 2 strips of the roasted red bell pepper, if using, in a crisscross fashion on top of the filling in each cup. Or sprinkle each with a tiny pinch of paprika, if desired. Place the filled cups on an ungreased baking sheet and bake for 8 to 10 minutes, or until heated through. Serve immediately.

5. If you are serving as a pâté, gently reheat before serving. Cut the baguette into rounds, spread with the pâté, and serve.

NOTE: White mushrooms can be used in place of some of the portobellos to stretch the rich portobello flavor.

TO ROAST PEPPERS: Preheat the oven to 400°F. Cut a small slit in each pepper and roast for 45 minutes. Remove from the oven and immediately wrap each pepper in plastic wrap. When the peppers have cooled, peel the skin from the flesh and remove the stems, ribs, and seeds. The peppers are easiest to peel after they have been refrigerated in the plastic wrap for 2 hours. Do not hold the peppers under running water, as this will wash away the intense flavor.

Smoky Pinto Pâté

This pâté is similar to refried beans but without the mess or elbow grease. Chipotle paste, miso, and tamari yield a smoky, meaty flavor. The pâté works equally well as a dip, a spread for bread or crackers, a side dish, or a burrito filling.

MAKES ABOUT 3 CUPS

1 cup dried pinto beans, sorted, rinsed well, and drained,
        or 2½ cups canned pinto beans, rinsed and drained
1 tablespoon olive oil
1 medium onion, chopped
¼ teaspoon sea salt
3 garlic cloves, minced
1 tablespoon plus 2 teaspoons red miso
1 tablespoon tamari
2 teaspoons Chipotle Paste (page 192)
1½ teaspoons fresh lime juice
¾ teaspoon dried oregano, crumbled
2 pinches ground cloves

1. If using dried beans, place them in a medium saucepan with enough cold water to cover by a few inches. Bring to a full boil, then boil for 3 to 5 minutes. Remove from the heat, cover, and let stand for 1 hour. (Alternatively, if you have the time, you can soak the beans at room temperature for at least 4 hours or overnight.) Rinse the beans and the saucepan thoroughly.

2. Return the beans to the saucepan, add 3 cups cold water, and bring to a boil. Reduce the heat to low, cover, and simmer, stirring occasionally, until tender, about 1½ hours. Drain.

3. Heat the oil in a medium skillet over medium-high heat. Add the onion and salt and sauté, stirring occasionally, until the onion is almost translucent, about 5 minutes. Add the garlic and sauté, stirring constantly, until the onion is translucent, about 2 minutes more.

4. Puree the beans, onion mixture, and ¼ cup plus 2 tablespoons water in a food processor or blender. Add the miso, tamari, chipotle paste, lime juice, oregano, and cloves. Puree, scraping down the sides, until smooth and creamy. Add water, 1 tablespoon at a time, if necessary, to thin the puree. Serve or refrigerate.

NOTE: The pâté can be made in advance and stored in the refrigerator for several days.

"To be free from obstacles means not to fight them, not to hate them. Be free from all obstacles, and do not allow thoughts to arise in the mind."

— Eido Roshi

THE CORNERS

While members of the Soto sect of Zen Buddhism sit and watch their breath during meditation, Rinzai Zen Buddhists work on puzzles, or koans. Koans, enigmatic stories that were written long ago, are used to help move students away from logical thinking into a more intuitive understanding. Many koans end with a Zen monk's attaining enlightenment upon hearing a word or a sound that causes something to be seen from a new angle. At first glance, koans seem impenetrable, such as the famous question, "What is the sound of one hand clapping?" And yet they can be quite helpful as we struggle with contemporary life's problems.

Our abbot, Eido Roshi, often selects a koan as the subject for his teishos, or formal talks. One such talk gave us all some insight. The first part went like this:

Smoke over the hill indicates fire. When you see horns on the other side of the fence, you know there is an ox there. Given one corner, you grasp the other three. One glance and you ought to discern even the smallest difference. This is the everyday matter of robed monks.

There are no "right" answers to koans, since it is best that each student reach an understanding without being told. In fact, visitors to Zen centers are often put off because there is little explanation of the how and why of things. We are "given one corner," and it is up to us to "grasp the other three," or we will not fully understand and appreciate what is in front of us.

In another talk, Roshi told us, "If the postage stamp is not straight, we can assume that the letter writer is not straight. . . . By seeing that one corner, at least three aspects of the person are revealed."

Some time after that, Hal, a young high school student, came to the monastery to spend a month on a work-study program. One day during a morning meeting, he revealed to the residents that his decision to come to the monastery was clinched when he received the reply to his inquiry letter. What impressed him was how neatly the stamp was placed on the envelope. Its placement spoke volumes to him about the monastery and what he would find when he got there. Hal had never heard Roshi's story about the postage stamp.

Even in the small act of placing a stamp on a letter, we reveal more than we realize, and we send a message that someone might be waiting and ready to hear.

—Myochi

Lentil-Walnut Pâté

This is a recipe adapted from one given to me by my friend Judy Kaestner, a professional chef. Upon tasting it, people are always surprised at its remarkable likeness to liver pâté. It's a perfect way to start a dinner party.

Serve a small bowl of Dijon mustard alongside the pâté. Spread a little Dijon on a cracker or bread and then a healthy serving of pâté.

MAKES ABOUT 3 CUPS

⅔ cup green lentils, sorted, rinsed well, and drained
2 tablespoons canola or corn oil
1 medium onion, diced
2 teaspoons sea salt, plus more to taste
4 garlic cloves, minced
1 tablespoon plus 2 teaspoons dried basil, crumbled
1 tablespoon plus 1 teaspoon dried thyme, crumbled
1 tablespoon dried oregano, crumbled
2 cups walnuts, toasted (see page 6)
2 tablespoons Dijon mustard
Freshly milled black pepper

1. Place 2 cups cold water and the lentils in a small saucepan and bring to a boil. Reduce the heat to low, cover, and simmer until tender, 30 to 40 minutes. It's OK if the lentils are a bit mushy. Do not drain. Set aside.

2. Heat the oil in a medium skillet over medium-high heat. Add the onion and salt and sauté, stirring occasionally, until the onion begins to soften, about 2 minutes. Add the garlic and herbs and sauté until the onion is translucent, 3 to 5 minutes more. Set aside to cool.

3. Place the walnuts in a food processor and process until well ground. Add the lentils and their cooking liquid, the onion mixture, mustard, and salt. Puree, scraping down the sides, until a smooth paste forms, 3 to 5 minutes. Season with pepper and additional salt, if desired, and serve.

Nondairy Taco Dip or Spread

What this dip lacks in fat, it more than makes up for in flavor. It's definitely worth making Chipotle Paste for this dip if you don't have any on hand. Serve with chips, with a Mexican-style menu, or use as a spread for sandwiches.

MAKES ABOUT 1¾ CUPS

1 pound soft tofu
2 tablespoons red miso
2 tablespoons fresh lemon juice
1 teaspoon Chipotle Paste (page 192)
½ teaspoon sea salt
2 pinches garlic powder

Place all the ingredients in a food processor or blender and puree, scraping down the sides, until smooth and creamy. Serve.

Chipotle Paste

I always keep a container of this paste in the refrigerator. It's a marvelous way to perk up a dish with a spicy, smoky flavor that suggests meat. Though I usually use whole chipotles, ground ones can also be used. There's plenty here to last you a while; a little goes a long way.

MAKES ABOUT ¼ CUP

8 whole dried chipotle peppers or 1 tablespoon plus
   1½ teaspoons ground chipotle
1 tablespoon fresh lemon juice
1 teaspoon ground cinnamon
½ teaspoon chili powder
½ teaspoon dried oregano, crumbled
2 pinches ground cloves

If using whole chipotles, place them in a small saucepan with just enough water to cover. Bring to a boil and boil for 30 minutes, adding more water if the saucepan threatens to dry out. Reserve the cooking liquid. (If there is none left, place 2 tablespoons hot water in the pan and swirl it to pick up the chipotle essence.) Remove and discard the stems from the chipotles. Place the chipotles and 2 tablespoons of the cooking liquid, the lemon juice, cinnamon, chili powder, oregano, and cloves in a food processor or blender. Puree, scraping down the sides, until smooth and creamy, 3 to 5 minutes.

If using ground chipotles, stir all the ingredients together in a small bowl with 2 tablespoons water to form a paste.

Refrigerate the paste in an airtight container. It will keep for at least 1 month.

Roasted Eggplant and Red Pepper Hummus

This is a lip-smacking, decadent hummus, usually reserved for celebration dinners and special events. The red peppers and eggplant can be roasted while the chickpeas are soaking and cooking. Though not quick to prepare, this spread can be made in advance. Serve with crackers or slices of sourdough baguette.

MAKES ABOUT 5 CUPS

1 cup dried chickpeas, sorted, rinsed well, and drained,
    or 2½ cups canned chickpeas, rinsed and drained
1 large eggplant (about 1 pound)
6 garlic cloves, peeled
4 medium red bell peppers, roasted (see page 185)
½ cup tahini
½ cup fresh lemon juice
2½ teaspoons sea salt, plus more to taste
½ teaspoon cumin seeds, toasted (see page 6) and
    ground

1. If using dried chickpeas, place them in a medium saucepan with enough cold water to cover by a few inches. Bring to a full boil and boil for 3 to 5 minutes. Remove from the heat, cover, and let stand for 1 hour. (Alternatively, if you have the time and foresight, you can soak the beans at room temperature for at least 4 hours or overnight.) Rinse the chickpeas and the saucepan thoroughly before continuing.

2. Return the chickpeas to the saucepan, add 3 cups cold water, and bring to a boil. Reduce the heat to low, cover, and simmer until tender, about 1 hour. Drain and set aside to cool.

3. Meanwhile, preheat the oven to 400°F. Pierce the eggplant a few times with a fork and roast for 1 hour, or until it collapses. Cool. Scrape the flesh from the skin into a medium bowl; discard the skin.

4. Mince the garlic in a food processor, scraping down the sides. Add the chickpeas, eggplant, and roasted peppers and puree. Add the tahini, lemon juice, salt, and cumin and puree until smooth and creamy. Taste and adjust the seasonings. Serve cold or at room temperature.

A slightly simpler version without the eggplant, this hummus is just as satisfying but a touch less complex.

MAKES ABOUT 3½ CUPS

VARIATION

Roasted Red Pepper Hummus

Proceed as directed, but omit the eggplant. Decrease the garlic to 3 cloves and use only 3 roasted red peppers. Decrease the lemon juice to ⅓ cup and the salt to 1¾ teaspoons.

MINDFUL EATING

How many of us pay full attention when we eat? Most of us eat on the run or as we're doing something else, like driving a car, watching the news, or reading a newspaper. When was the last time that you actually sat down to a meal, took the time to appreciate what you were about to eat, and were mindful of every bite? It might be so long ago that you've forgotten, but you once knew how to eat this way without thinking.

All infants eat mindfully. Just watch any baby drink a bottle or nurse at its mother's breast. If distracted, it stops eating until the distraction disappears. As adults, we've learned to do two things at once, but we do neither of them very well. It will take some practice to return to your child mind, but the bliss that you once experienced while eating can be yours again.

The Five Reflections, which are chanted before each meal, bring our attention to our work and the work of others, heightening our awareness of the act of eating. And although we may be very hungry when we sit down to eat, these prayers give us pause. Before we eat, we place the equivalent of seven grains of rice on a board that is passed down the table. After the meal, the offering is taken outdoors and put at the foot of a statue of the Bodhisattva of Compassion. The animals that live in the mountains around the monastery — deer, chipmunks, squirrels — help themselves to this food. This offering symbolizes our desire to share what we have. It brings our attention to the fact that in this moment we have all we need, and more.

This mindful approach can be transferred into all activities of our lives.

— Myochi

Bahumbagamus

We often serve this cross between baba ghanoush and hummus for supper with freshly baked bread.

MAKES ABOUT 5¾ CUPS

1   cup dried chickpeas, sorted, rinsed well, and drained,
        or 2½ cups canned chickpeas, rinsed and drained
2   medium eggplants (2–2½ pounds total)
6   garlic cloves, peeled
¾   cup tahini
½   cup plus 2 tablespoons fresh lemon juice
2½ teaspoons sea salt, plus more to taste
2   teaspoons tamari
1   teaspoon freshly milled black pepper
¼   teaspoon cayenne pepper, plus more to taste

1. If using dried chickpeas, place them in a medium saucepan with enough cold water to cover by a few inches. Bring to a full boil, then boil for 3 to 5 minutes. Remove from the heat, cover, and let stand for 1 hour. (Alternatively, if you have the time, you can soak the beans at room temperature for at least 4 hours or overnight.) Rinse the chickpeas and the saucepan thoroughly.

2. Return the chickpeas to the saucepan, add 3 cups cold water, and bring to a boil. Reduce the heat to low, cover, and simmer until tender, about 1 hour. Drain and set aside to cool.

3. Meanwhile, preheat the oven to 400°F. Pierce the eggplants a few times with a fork and roast for about 1 hour, or until they collapse. Cool. Scrape the flesh from the skins into a medium bowl; discard the skins.

4. Mince the garlic in a food processor, scraping down the sides. Add the chickpeas and eggplant and puree. Add the tahini, lemon juice, salt, tamari, black pepper, and cayenne and puree until smooth and creamy. Taste and adjust the seasonings, adding more cayenne and salt, if necessary. Refrigerate or serve immediately.

NOTE: The spread is best if made in advance and refrigerated for a few hours.

Miso– Peanut Butter Sauce

When I first saw a Japanese monk mixing peanut butter with miso, I thought it was a strange combination. However, I was pleasantly surprised when I tasted it. Guests always love the sauce and are curious to know what's in it. Because its complex taste insinuates an elaborate preparation, they are amazed at its simplicity.

The monk served this sauce tossed with steamed fresh green beans. While that combination has remained a favorite of the residents, the sauce also goes well with asparagus or broccoli. Many of the residents like the sauce so much that they put it on rice, pasta, and many other foods.

MAKES ABOUT 2 CUPS

¾ cup peanut butter
½ cup white miso
2 tablespoons honey

Place all the ingredients in a medium bowl with ½ cup hot water. Whisk together well. Add up to ¼ cup more water to reach the desired consistency. Serve.

NOTES: If you'd like the sauce to be sweeter, add a little more honey. Use smooth or chunky peanut butter. I use whatever is open at the time.

I usually toss this sauce with vegetables that have been steamed or boiled and then briefly shocked in cold water. The heat generated by the hot vegetables thins the sauce and quickly sends it to the bottom of the serving dish. If you want to toss it with hot vegetables, use less water. When I serve the sauce with hot vegetables, I usually put it on the side and let each person spoon the sauce over his or her own portion of vegetables.

Try red miso or a combination of red and white. You may also want to use another sweetener: maple syrup, brown rice syrup, or barley malt, for example.

Premium Basil Pesto

This creamy pesto is made with walnuts instead of the traditional, more expensive pine nuts. I make it in the summer with fresh basil from our garden. I toss the pesto with pasta, usually penne, in advance and serve at room temperature. Pesto can also be mixed with vegetables, used as a base for a salad dressing, or spread on good-quality crusty bread.

MAKES ABOUT 3¼ CUPS

9 garlic cloves, minced
1 cup walnuts, toasted (see page 6)
3 cups tightly packed fresh basil leaves
1½ cups extra-virgin olive oil
1¼ cups freshly grated Parmesan or Asiago cheese
1¼ teaspoons sea salt

Mince the garlic in a food processor, scraping down the sides. Add the walnuts and process until well ground, scraping down the sides. Add the basil, then the olive oil, and process until the basil is chopped, scraping down the sides. Add the cheese and salt and puree for about 2 minutes, or until smooth and creamy. Refrigerate or serve immediately.

NOTES: If you refrigerate the pesto for later use, bring it to room temperature before using.

I generally use 1 to 1½ cups pesto for 1 pound pasta.

Leftover pesto can be frozen and is still fresh-tasting months later.

Scallion-Tamari Mayonnaise

I usually serve this mayonnaise with vegetables such as broccoli or asparagus. It can also be mixed into rice, served as a dip for crudités, or used as a salad dressing. A little goes a long way.

MAKES ABOUT ½ CUP

½ cup mayonnaise
2 teaspoons tamari
2 scallions, very thinly sliced on the diagonal
   (see page 45)

Whisk together the mayonnaise and tamari in a small bowl. Fold in the scallions. Refrigerate for 2 hours and serve.

Citrus Tamari

This slightly sweet, seasoned variation of tamari is delectable served with tofu or used as a salad dressing or in place of tamari as a dipping sauce.

MAKES ABOUT ¾ CUP

½ cup tamari
1 tablespoon plus 1 teaspoon honey
1 tablespoon fresh lemon juice
1½ teaspoons rice vinegar
¼ teaspoon sea salt

Combine all the ingredients in a jar and shake well until the salt dissolves. (Alternatively, you can place the ingredients in a bowl and whisk vigorously until the salt dissolves.) Serve.

Garden Brown Sauce

This ultimate vegetarian brown sauce is the creation of Steve Petusevsky. I made it for one of our Thanksgiving feasts, and I've been cooking it ever since. It has an unexpectedly meatlike flavor, and can be used as the base for other sauces, soups, stews, or curries. Serve with Nondairy Mashed Potatoes (page 102), Quinoa-Mushroom Nut Loaf (page 86), Quinoa-Sunflower Stuffing (page 88), or anything else with which you would traditionally serve gravy.

MAKES ABOUT 4 CUPS

2 tablespoons olive oil
2 large carrots, chopped
¾ medium onion, chopped
2 large celery ribs, chopped
2 ounces white mushrooms, cut into ¼-inch-thick slices (about 1 cup)
4 garlic cloves, halved
¼ cup tomato paste
¼ cup unbleached white flour
1 cup dry red wine
2 tablespoons tamari
2 teaspoons peppercorns
3 bay leaves
1 teaspoon dried thyme, crumbled
½ teaspoon sea salt

1. Heat the oil in a medium saucepan over medium-high heat. Add the carrots and onion and sauté, stirring occasionally, until lightly browned, about 15 minutes.

2. Add the celery, mushrooms, and garlic and sauté, stirring occasionally, until browned, about 10 minutes more.

3. Add the tomato paste and sauté until browned, about 10 minutes. Add the flour and cook, stirring constantly, for 1 minute.

4. Stir in the wine and scrape up the browned bits from the bottom of the saucepan. Add 6 cups water and the remaining ingredients and bring to a boil. Reduce the heat to low and simmer for 45 minutes.

5. Strain through a very fine sieve into a medium bowl; discard the solids. Serve immediately or refrigerate for up to 1 week. Make a double batch and freeze any leftovers. The sauce can be frozen for up to 3 months.

Tahini-Applesauce Spread

Our pantry is always stocked with tahini and applesauce, so this spread is a breeze to make. This is the quintessential spread for Cinnamon-Currant Bread (page 168), and it goes well with most other baked goods.

MAKES ABOUT 1 CUP

½ cup tahini
½ cup unsweetened applesauce

Place the tahini and applesauce in a food processor and puree until well blended, scraping down the sides. Add more applesauce if you want a sweeter spread or more tahini if you prefer a stronger tahini flavor.

Tahini-Miso Sauce

This subtle sauce is a good alternative to butter on muffins and yeast breads. It's also great as a topping for vegetables or tossed with a green salad.

MAKES ABOUT 2 CUPS

1 cup tahini
¼ cup plus 2 tablespoons white miso
1 teaspoon fresh lemon juice
1 teaspoon tamari
   Maple syrup (optional)

Puree all the ingredients, except the maple syrup, if using, with ½ cup plus 2 tablespoons hot water in a food processor or blender, scraping down the sides. (Alternatively, you can whisk the ingredients in a bowl until smooth and well blended.) Add the maple syrup to taste, if using.

GRATITUDE

DESSERT IS RARELY OFFERED AT DAI BOSATSU ZENDO, AND USUALLY ONLY FOR celebration dinners. When we do serve it, we sometimes go over the top. What's life without an occasional venture out-of-bounds?

Though none of the recipes in the rest of the book call for refined sugar, you'll find it in some of the recipes that follow, in downright decadent desserts. In other cases, where the flavor and quality would be unaffected, I have lowered the fat or replaced refined sugar with honey and/or maple syrup.

Whether it's low-fat Coconut-Pecan Carrot Cake or outrageously rich Samsara Cheesecake, these desserts all have one thing in common: they are indisputably delicious.

—Seppo

Double-Berry Poached Pears

Poached in a delicious brew of cranberries, wine, and strawberries, these sweet-tart pears emerge bright red. The poaching liquid is then reduced to make a sauce to serve with the pears. With the bright red color and hints of green and white, this dessert is spectacular for the holidays, but it can transform any meal into a special occasion.

MAKES 10 SERVINGS

1   12-ounce bag fresh or frozen cranberries, sorted, rinsed well, and drained
1   pint fresh strawberries, hulled, or one 12-ounce bag frozen strawberries
1   cup dry red wine
¼   cup plus 3 tablespoons maple syrup
¼   cup fresh lemon juice
10 Anjou, Bartlett, or Bosc pears

Vanilla Whipped Cream (optional; page 218)

1. Place 2 cups water, the cranberries, strawberries, wine, maple syrup, and lemon juice in a medium pot and bring to a boil. Reduce the heat to low, cover, and simmer until the berries have softened considerably and the cranberries have split, about 10 minutes. Remove from the heat. Using a potato masher or the back of a large spoon, mash the berries until they have mostly dissolved into the poaching liquid.

2. Peel the first pear, leaving its stem intact. Slice across the base, well below the widest point, just enough that the pear will stand solidly upright. Immediately place the pear in the poaching liquid to prevent discoloring; if necessary, spoon some of the liquid over it to make sure it is entirely covered. Continue with the remaining pears.

3. Cover the pot and place it over medium-low heat. Just before it comes to a boil, reduce the heat to very low and simmer, stirring occasionally, until the pears are tender, 15 to 30 minutes, depending on ripeness. Do not boil.

4. Remove from the heat and let the pears cool in the poaching liquid. Once the pot is cool, place it in the refrigerator for a few hours

or overnight. The longer the pears sit in the poaching liquid, the more flavor they will absorb. Or serve immediately.

5. Transfer the pears to a plate and bring the poaching liquid to a simmer over medium-low heat. Simmer, stirring occasionally, until thick and syrupy, 20 to 30 minutes. Cool.

6. Serve the pears cold or at room temperature with the sauce and vanilla whipped cream, if using.

NOTES: It doesn't matter whether the pears are ripe and luscious or still a bit unripe. They will absorb the poaching liquid and soften. Poaching is also a good remedy when you have a bowlful of pears that are ripening faster than you can eat them. Poached pears store well and can be refrigerated for up to a week before serving. The poaching liquid, served with sour cream, makes a delicious topping for waffles or pancakes, or mix it into yogurt for a special treat.

Buy extra bags of cranberries when they are in season and store them in the freezer.

Hummingbird Pound Cake

This fragrant, moist, fruit-filled variation on a southern classic doesn't contain the ingredients usually associated with pound cake, but its texture is similarly dense.

MAKES 1 BUNDT OR 9-X-13-INCH CAKE

WET INGREDIENTS

  2 cups mashed ripe bananas
1½ cups plus 2 tablespoons unsweetened applesauce
  1 cup crushed pineapple, well drained
  ½ cup plus 1 tablespoon honey
  ½ cup maple syrup
  2 large eggs
  2 tablespoons canola or corn oil
1½ teaspoons vanilla extract

DRY INGREDIENTS

  3 cups whole wheat pastry flour or unbleached white
      flour
  2 teaspoons ground cinnamon
  1 teaspoon baking soda
  1 teaspoon sea salt
  1 cup chopped walnuts or pecans, toasted (see page 6)

    Vanilla Whipped Cream (page 218)

1. Preheat the oven to 325°F. Coat a bundt pan or a 9-x-13-inch baking dish with spray, oil, or butter and set aside.

2. Whisk together all the wet ingredients in a large bowl.

3. In a medium bowl, combine all the dry ingredients thoroughly.

4. Add the dry ingredients to the wet and whisk just until they are evenly combined, using as few strokes as possible. Fold in the walnuts or pecans.

5. Pour the batter into the baking pan or dish and spread evenly. Bake for 1 hour and 10 minutes for a bundt pan, or 1 hour and 35 minutes for a baking dish, until the cake is browned and a toothpick inserted in the center comes out clean. Let cool for 10 minutes before removing from the pan. Cool completely on a rack. Frost with vanilla whipped cream and serve.

"Besides sitting, Zen requires spirit — vital, dynamic spirit. It's not only a matter of being quiet — that's not what Zen is. POW! POW! Even striking the hand and sounding the clappers in the zendo are no other than

THIS!

Just at the right moment, not too soon, not too late — strike! POW! POW! Strike with intensity! Then, with this sound, someone may realize THIS."

—Eido Roshi

Samsara Cheesecake

This is the very best homemade cheesecake we've ever tasted — dense, creamy, and cheesy. It tastes even better the next day, so make it in advance if time allows. Serve plain, drizzled with the reduced liquid from Double-Berry Poached Pears (page 204), strawberry sauce (see page 212), or hot fudge.

MAKES 12 TO 16 SERVINGS

CRUST
- 1 cup pecans or walnuts, ground
- ½ cup wheat germ
- 2 pinches ground cinnamon
- Pinch ground ginger
- 1 tablespoon maple syrup

CHEESECAKE
- 1½ pounds cream cheese, at room temperature
- 1 cup ricotta cheese, at room temperature, preferably pureed in a food processor
- 4 large eggs
- ¼ cup plus 1 tablespoon honey
- 3 tablespoons maple syrup
- 1 tablespoon vanilla extract
- 1 tablespoon grated lemon zest
- 2 pinches sea salt

1. Preheat the oven to 350°F. Coat the bottom of a 9-inch spring-form pan with spray, oil, or butter.

2. CRUST: Combine the nuts, wheat germ, cinnamon, and ginger in a medium bowl. Add the maple syrup and mix until evenly distributed. Press into the bottom of the pan and bake for 15 minutes. Set aside to cool.

3. CHEESECAKE: Combine the cream cheese, ricotta, eggs, honey, maple syrup, vanilla, lemon zest, and salt with an electric mixer, scraping the bowl with a rubber spatula when necessary, until the cheeses are creamed and completely mixed with the other ingredients.

4. Pour the cheesecake batter into the crust and bake for 50 minutes, or until the outer rim of the cake looks cooked but the center is still soft and wobbly. Don't be afraid to remove it from the oven; it will firm as it cools. Place on a rack and let cool to room temperature for about 2 hours, then refrigerate for at least 3 hours more.

NOTES: I often serve this cheesecake garnished with a ring of fresh mint sprigs around its base and one or two sprigs together on the top. If you have a lot of mint growing near your house, this is a great way to use it.

When I'm in a rush, I sometimes refrigerate the cheesecake almost directly from the oven. That works, but don't be surprised if cracks form. A sprig of mint in each crack will help to cover it up.

Coconut-Pecan Carrot Cake with Orange–Cream Cheese Frosting

I've tried many recipes for carrot cake over the years and have never been satisfied. When I had to bake a cake for a special occasion at the monastery, I created this reduced-fat version. To make the cake even more wholesome, I replaced the white flour with whole wheat flour, replaced the white sugar with maple syrup and honey, and added toasted wheat germ. The result is not only scrumptious but healthful.

MAKES ONE 9-X-13-INCH CAKE

2 cups whole wheat pastry flour
¾ cup wheat germ, toasted (see page 6)
2 teaspoons baking powder
2 teaspoons baking soda
1 teaspoon ground cinnamon
1 teaspoon sea salt
1¼ cups unsweetened applesauce
½ cup honey
½ cup maple syrup
4 large egg whites plus 1 large egg, or 3 large eggs
2 teaspoons vanilla extract
2 teaspoons grated orange zest
3½ cups packed grated carrots
1 cup chopped pecans or walnuts, toasted (see page 6)
½ cup shredded unsweetened coconut, toasted (see page 6)
⅓ cup dried currants (optional)

Orange–Cream Cheese Frosting (page 211)

1. Preheat the oven to 350°F. Coat a 9-x-13-inch baking dish with spray, oil, or butter and set aside.

2. Combine the flour, wheat germ, baking powder, baking soda, cinnamon, and salt thoroughly in a medium bowl.

3. Combine the applesauce, honey, and maple syrup with an electric mixer in a large bowl. Add the egg whites and egg(s) and beat for 30 seconds, or until frothy. Add the vanilla and orange zest and beat for a few seconds more.

4. Stir the flour mixture into the applesauce mixture just until thoroughly blended. Fold in the carrots, pecans or walnuts, coconut, and currants, if using.

5. Pour the batter into the baking dish and spread evenly. Bake for 45 to 50 minutes, or until the cake is golden brown and a toothpick inserted in the center comes out clean. Let cool for 10 minutes before removing from the pan. Cool completely on a rack before frosting. Serve.

NOTE: An equal amount of whole wheat flour or unbleached white flour may be substituted for the pastry flour.

Orange–Cream Cheese Frosting

This is the classic frosting for carrot cake. For a nondairy version, use one batch of Orange Nondairy Whipped Cream (page 220), but don't frost the cake until just before serving. If the frosting is too sweet, it hides the subtle undertones of the cake, so be careful not to add too much honey.

12 ounces cream cheese, at room temperature
     About 2 tablespoons honey, or to taste
2½ teaspoons vanilla extract
2½ teaspoons grated orange zest or 1 teaspoon orange
        extract

Beat all the ingredients together with an electric mixer until smooth. Spread on the cooled cake.

NOTES: Sprinkling toasted coconut and/or arranging toasted pecan halves on top of the frosting makes an impressive presentation.
    If you are serving a large crowd, make two cakes and layer frosting between them.

Strawberry-Banana Layer Cake

This fruit-filled cake tastes remarkably like strawberry shortcake with bananas. It can be served frosted or unfrosted for a birthday or other special occasion.

MAKES 12 TO 16 SERVINGS

BANANA CAKE

2¼ cups whole wheat pastry flour or unbleached white flour
 1 teaspoon baking soda
 1 teaspoon baking powder
 ½ teaspoon sea salt
1¼ cups mashed ripe bananas
 1 cup low-fat buttermilk or plain low-fat yogurt
 2 large eggs
 2 tablespoons canola or corn oil
1½ teaspoons grated lemon zest
 1 teaspoon vanilla extract

STRAWBERRY SAUCE

 2 pints strawberries, hulled and halved if large
 2 tablespoons honey
 2 tablespoons maple syrup
1½ teaspoons fresh lemon juice
 ½ teaspoon vanilla extract

 2 ripe bananas, mashed

   Double batch Vanilla Whipped Cream (page 218) or Nondairy Whipped Cream (page 220; optional)
   Halved strawberries, for garnish (if frosting is used)

1. BANANA CAKE: Preheat the oven to 350°F. Coat two 8-inch square cake pans or two 9-inch round cake pans with spray, oil, or butter.

2. Combine the flour, baking soda, baking powder, and salt in a large bowl.

3. In a medium bowl, whisk together the bananas, buttermilk or yogurt, eggs, oil, lemon zest, and vanilla. Add to the flour mixture and mix just until evenly blended.

4. Divide the batter between the two baking pans and bake for about 30 minutes, or until golden brown and a toothpick inserted in the center comes out clean. Place the pans on a rack and let cool for 10 minutes before removing the cakes from the pans. Allow the cakes to cool completely on the rack.

5. STRAWBERRY SAUCE: Puree 1 pint of the strawberries in a food processor with the honey, maple syrup, lemon juice, and vanilla until smooth. Add the remaining 1 pint strawberries and pulse until chopped but not liquefied.

6. Cut each cake in half horizontally, to make 4 layers. An easy way to do this evenly is to first cut each round cake into 2 half-circles and then slice each half-circle into 2 layers. Or, if using square pans, cut each cake in half vertically and then slice each half horizontally. The slice mark is easily covered with whipped cream and strawberry sauce.

7. Place the bottom layer on a serving platter. Spoon about one-third of the strawberry sauce on that layer. (If frosting the cake, use half of the strawberry sauce.) Place the second layer on the strawberry sauce and cover it evenly with the mashed bananas. Place the third layer on the bananas and cover it with another one-third or one-half of the strawberry sauce. Put the top layer in place.

8. If desired, frost with the vanilla whipped cream or nondairy whipped cream, if using. Press the strawberry halves into the frosting. If using vanilla whipped cream, you can frost and refrigerate the cake for up to 2 hours before serving. If using nondairy whipped cream, frost the cake just before serving, since the topping will discolor within an hour or so. If you are not going to frost the cake, pour the remaining one-third of the strawberry sauce over the cake before serving.

THE OFFERING BOARD

The last thing to make its way down the table at mealtime is the offering board. The equivalent of seven grains of rice that we each place on this board symbolizes our willingness to share what we have with others, our gratitude for that which we have, and our desire to satisfy the hungry ghost spirit that resides in each of us.

This hungry ghost represents our cravings. In Buddhism, the ghost, considered to be one of six modes of existence, is depicted as a being with a huge belly and a tiny mouth who suffers the torment of hunger. It is said that greed, envy, and jealousy in this life can lead to rebirth as a hungry ghost. Since the human mode is the only one in which it's possible to attain enlightenment, we express gratitude for being human even with all our faults, shortcomings, and cravings.

The food tastes all the more satisfying for this realization. Before we eat, our offering is placed on the altar. After the meal, it is carried outside and placed at the foot of a statue of the Bodhisattva of Compassion for the animals that live in the woods.

—Myochi

Oatmeal-Raisin Pudding

This dish was born of a need to use up leftover oatmeal. Guests put in special requests for it — not realizing, of course, that it is made from breakfast. It has a comforting caramel flavor.

MAKES 6 TO 8 SERVINGS

2 cups cooked old-fashioned rolled oats
1 teaspoon grated lemon zest
½ teaspoon ground cinnamon
¾ cup milk, soy milk, or rice milk
2 large eggs, lightly whisked
3 tablespoons honey
1 teaspoon vanilla extract
½ cup raisins

Vanilla Whipped Cream or Cinnamon-Mocha Whipped Cream (page 218; optional)

1. Preheat the oven to 350°F. Coat an 8-inch square baking dish with spray, oil, or butter and set aside.

2. Whisk together the oatmeal, lemon zest, and cinnamon in a large bowl. Whisk in the milk, eggs, honey, and vanilla until thoroughly incorporated. Fold in the raisins.

3. Pour the oatmeal mixture into the baking dish. Bake for 1 hour, or until the top of the pudding begins to brown and is somewhat firm (the center should still be a little soft). The pudding will set further once it begins to cool. Serve hot, at room temperature, or chilled, with whipped cream on the side, if desired.

Basmati Rice Pudding with Tropical Fruit

This is an exotic way to use basmati rice, and you may already have all the fruit for it in your pantry. The versatile treat can be served for breakfast or dessert. Top with a spoonful of slightly sweetened whipped cream or pour a bit of milk over the pudding.

MAKES 8 TO 16 SERVINGS

2½ cups cooked white or brown basmati rice (from about ¾ cup uncooked rice)
1 20-ounce can crushed pineapple, drained of 1 cup juice
¾ cup raisins
½ cup shredded unsweetened coconut, toasted (see page 6)
2 cups milk, soy milk, or rice milk
¾ cup mashed ripe banana
½ cup light brown sugar
2 large eggs, lightly whisked
1 teaspoon almond extract
½ teaspoon ground cinnamon
⅛ teaspoon sea salt

1. Preheat the oven to 350°F. Coat an 11-x-13-inch baking dish with spray, oil, or butter.

2. Combine the rice, pineapple, raisins, and coconut in a large bowl.

3. Whisk together the milk, banana, brown sugar, eggs, almond extract, cinnamon, and salt in a medium bowl. Add to the rice mixture and mix well.

4. Pour the rice mixture into the baking dish and bake for 45 minutes, or until set. Serve hot, at room temperature, or chilled.

Rice Porridge Pudding

This rice pudding is a great way to use up leftover Rice Porridge. Either Nondairy Whipped Cream (page 220) or Cinnamon-Mocha Whipped Cream (page 218) makes a superb topping.

MAKES 4 TO 8 SERVINGS

2 cups Rice Porridge (page 5)
1 teaspoon grated lemon zest
½ teaspoon ground cinnamon
⅛ teaspoon sea salt
¾ cup milk, soy milk, or rice milk
¾ cup honey
4 large eggs, lightly whisked
1 teaspoon vanilla extract
½ cup raisins

1. Preheat the oven to 350°F. Coat an 8-inch square baking dish with spray, oil, or butter and set aside.

2. Whisk together the rice porridge, lemon zest, cinnamon, and salt in a large bowl.

3. Whisk the milk, honey, eggs, and vanilla into the rice-porridge mixture. Fold in the raisins.

4. Pour into the baking dish and bake for 1 hour, or until almost set. The center may still be a bit soft, but it will firm as it cools. Serve hot, warm, at room temperature, or chilled.

Cinnamon-Mocha Whipped Cream

This flavored whipped cream will enhance almost any dessert. It's so good that people are willing to eat it directly from the bowl.

MAKES ABOUT 2 CUPS

1 cup heavy cream
1½–2 tablespoons honey
1 teaspoon unsweetened cocoa
½ teaspoon instant coffee, crushed
½ teaspoon vanilla extract
2 pinches ground cinnamon

Place a nonmetal bowl in the freezer for 15 to 20 minutes. Pour the cream into the chilled bowl, then add the remaining ingredients. Beat with an electric mixer on high speed until the cream thickens and stiffens, 2 to 3 minutes. Refrigerate or serve immediately.

VARIATION

Vanilla Whipped Cream
If you're looking for a neutral topping that's alluring enough to make you lick the bowl, this is it.

1 cup heavy cream
1 tablespoon plus 1 teaspoon honey
2 teaspoons maple syrup
¾ teaspoon vanilla extract

Follow the instructions for Cinnamon-Mocha Whipped Cream.

NOTES: If you overwhip the cream so that it begins to turn buttery, gently whisk in additional cream, 1 tablespoon at a time. Do not beat the cream again.

Avoid using metal serving utensils and bowls, as they will destabilize the whipped cream.

SITTING ZAZEN

One can be taught how to sit zazen, but to be zazen is another matter. This state cannot be taught, and the most direct path to it is by "just sitting." Paradoxically, each one of us is being zazen at each moment. The trouble is that most of us don't realize this, and we sit zazen in order to gain this realization.

Just sitting has its own challenges. Though it may be simple to sit, concentrate on your breath, and not move, it is not easy. In the zendo, the meditation hall where sitting zazen is practiced, there are strict and what seem to the beginner rigid standards. Once you assume your sitting posture, the rule is "do not move until the jikijitsu, the head monk of the zendo, rings his bell." Generally the period of sitting lasts about forty-five minutes. If a group of beginners is visiting, the signal for a break is given after twenty minutes, allowing the participants to adjust their posture or stand quietly at their place for about five minutes. Then everyone resumes sitting. If there is restlessness—and, because of the robes that are worn, even the slightest movement makes a lot of noise—the jikijitsu might shout, "Silence!" or "Don't move!" or "Keep still!" Or he or she might sharply bang a wooden stick on the wooden floor—just once, to wake us up, to remind us to stop daydreaming! If we have been moving, we take this warning personally. It is not personal. We must remind ourselves that it is for the benefit of all. We bring our attention back to our breath as we were taught, and continue on.

—Myochi

Nondairy Whipped Cream

With tofu as the base, this topping is both delicious and healthful. It goes well with any dessert.

MAKES ABOUT 2½ CUPS

1   pound extra-firm tofu
1½ tablespoons honey
1   tablespoon maple syrup
1   tablespoon vanilla extract
2   teaspoons grated lemon zest
½   teaspoon sea salt

Puree the tofu in a food processor or blender just until it starts to break down. Add the honey, maple syrup, and vanilla. Puree, scraping down the sides, until smooth and creamy. Transfer to a medium bowl, mix in the lemon zest and salt, and serve immediately or refrigerate before serving.

VARIATIONS

Lemon Nondairy Whipped Cream
Prepare the recipe as directed, adding 1 teaspoon lemon extract.

Orange Nondairy Whipped Cream
Prepare the recipe as directed, replacing the lemon zest with 2 teaspoons grated orange zest and adding 1 teaspoon orange extract.

A monk visited the Chinese Zen master Joshu. Joshu asked him, "Have you been here before?"

The monk replied, "No, I haven't."

Joshu said, "Have a cup of tea."

Another monk came to visit Joshu, and Joshu asked him the same question: "Have you been here before?"

This monk replied, "Yes, I have."

Joshu said, "Have a cup of tea."

Joshu's attendant monk was puzzled and asked, "Master, the first monk said he'd never been here, and the second said he had. They are different, and yet you treated them both equally by offering them a cup of tea. Why is this so?"

Joshu replied, "Have a cup of tea."

—From *Joshuro Ku*,
translated by
Eido Roshi

WATER

SOME VARIETY OF BEVERAGE IS ALWAYS SERVED AT INFORMAL LUNCHES OR dinners at the monastery. For brunch, I sometimes make hot apple cider and pass it with coffee and a selection of teas. If there is a cold making its rounds, I often put out a big pot of Honey-Lemon Ginger Tea. The residents are comforted if not actually cured by its healing qualities.

I serve pitchers of fresh lemon water all through the year when I want to give the residents something cold. The recipe is so basic that I hesitate to mention it, but guests constantly ask for it. It simply consists of 2 tablespoons of fresh lemon juice mixed into 8 cups of water, with lemon slices added. Especially in the hot summer months, it's a quick and invitingly cool refreshment.

—Seppo

Honey-Lemon Ginger Tea

I often make a big pot of this tea and keep it warm on the stove all day. It's very soothing to sore throats and congested chests. It's also so refreshing that we enjoy it on a regular basis. The lemon and honey soften the edge of the ginger. Add as much or as little honey as you like.

MAKES ABOUT 4 CUPS

1 2½-inch piece ginger, halved lengthwise, and cut crosswise into ¼-inch-thick slices
   Juice of 1 large lemon (about ¼ cup)
2–4 tablespoons honey

Place the ginger and 4 cups cold water in a teapot or saucepan, cover, and bring to a boil. Reduce the heat to low and simmer for 20 to 30 minutes. Strain the tea, reserving the ginger for use another time, if you want. Add the lemon juice and honey to taste. Reheat and serve hot.

NOTE: The reserved ginger can be used for additional tea. Place more cold water over it, bring to a boil, and simmer again. The second tea will not be as strong, so you will need to use judgment when seasoning with lemon juice and honey.

THE LESSONS OF TEA

Whenever our abbot, Eido Roshi, has special visitors at the monastery, he has his attendant monk prepare tea for him and his guests. Sometimes the guests are treated to *sho no kiwami* tea — a rare tea that is harvested once a year in the mountains of Kyushu, the southern island of Japan. Roshi calls this tea "better than ultimate." It cannot be bought in this country, and even in Japan it is not easy to come by. As his attendant makes the tea, Roshi gives a lesson on how drinking it teaches us generosity, patience, and nonattachment.

Generosity. Since this is such a rare and expensive tea, we might be tempted to stint on the amount used for each serving. But because it is special, it is important to be generous with the portions to maximize the enjoyment of its unusual and rewarding taste.

Patience. The making of this tea cannot be rushed. It begins with a generous portion of tea leaves and water that is tepid, not boiling hot. Rather than being allowed to steep, the tea is poured into the waiting cups, poured back into the pot, back into the cups, and back into the pot, three or four times. Then it is ready to drink — just the right temperature, just the right depth of flavor. Just the right amount of time spent in preparation.

Nonattachment. The first sip is an explosion of flavor — powerful and subtle at the same time. The taste doesn't fade. We long for more. But a second cup would disappoint in comparison to the first. If we practice nonattachment and stop after the first cup, we will be rewarded with the lingering taste in our mouths for quite a while longer.

Generosity, patience, nonattachment. The lessons of tea, the essential spirit of Zen practice.

—Myochi

Umeboshi Tea

This is a traditional Japanese brew, said to bring good health if consumed in small quantities on a daily basis. Though we rarely partake of this exquisitely delicate tea, we deeply appreciate it when we do. It whets appetites before an Asian lunch or dinner and works equally well as a palate cleanser at the end of a meal.

MAKES 1½ CUPS

2 good-quality umeboshi plums

Remove the pits from the plums with your fingers and a small knife, scraping as much pulp as possible from the pits. Mash the plums in a small bowl with the back of a spoon until the skins are mashed into the pulp. Place in a teapot or small saucepan with 1½ cups boiling water. Stir well. Serve.

SAREI: THE TEA-DRINKING CEREMONY

Each day during the seven-day retreat of sesshin, there are two tea times, the first after morning service and the second at the beginning of the afternoon's first sit. In the morning, there is a choice of black tea or coffee. Green tea is served only in the afternoon.

Form and ritual go hand in hand in the monastery, especially during sesshin and most of all during sarei, the tea ceremony. The jisha and the jikijitsu strike their bells and clap their clappers in a special rhythm that signals the beginning and the end of this ceremony. Though it is not nearly as elaborate as the traditional Japanese tea ceremony, there is a formality to it. There is even a proper way to hold one's cup while drinking, with the fingers of the left hand tucked under the cup and the fingers of the right wrapped loosely around it.

After the instruments are sounded, two monks walk to the altar in the front of the zendo, carrying teapots in front of them, above their heads. They bow to the altar, where a cup sits empty and ready for the offering of tea. After pouring tea into the altar cup, the monks bow again and then proceed to serve us, Roshi first. As they near our seats, we raise our cups two by two and signal when to stop pouring by raising one palm. Silence is always maintained. We set our teacups down in front of us until everyone has been served. After Roshi picks up his cup and begins to drink, we each pick up our own cups, but not before the person in front of us. A wave of raised teacups begins at the altar and moves to the rear of the zendo. Once we are finished drinking, which is done quickly, we wait to set down our cups until our neighbor has set down his — another synchronized wave. By the third or fourth day of sesshin week, we are in such a groove that we are like one person taking and drinking tea.

—Myochi

Rosemary Apple Cider

This drink is welcome on a brisk autumn day and is a refreshing way to start off a dinner party in the colder months. The woodsy flavor of rosemary blends perfectly with the sweetness of the cider.

MAKES ½ GALLON

½ gallon apple cider
1 sprig fresh rosemary (about 6 inches long)

Place the cider and rosemary in a large saucepan, cover, and bring to a boil. Remove from the heat and let steep, covered, for 15 to 20 minutes. Remove and discard the rosemary and serve warm.

"Pain is the most difficult problem during sesshin. There are many methods for overcoming pain: this exercise or that mental attitude. But nothing works all the time, except perseverance. Perseverance not only reduces the degree of pain, but by itself it is a wonderful practice for perfecting the virtue of endurance."

— Eido Roshi

INCENSE

Incense greets us in every room and around every corner in the monastery. Rather than smell it, we are encouraged to listen to it burn. Just as there is an art to serving tea, flower arranging, and calligraphy, there is an art to burning incense. A sixteenth-century Zen priest is credited with describing the ten virtues of incense burning:

1. Incense burning opens the mind to divinity.
2. Incense burning purifies the mind and body.
3. Incense burning divests the mind of worldly impurities.
4. Incense burning wakes up the mind and keeps one alert.
5. Incense burning encourages the mind in solitude.
6. Incense burning brings peace to a busy mind.
7. One cannot burn too much incense.
8. Even a little incense is enough.
9. The age of the incense does not affect its efficacy.
10. Habitual use of incense causes no harm.

—Myochi

Tamarind Apple Cider

This simple variation of apple cider has an East Indian flair.

MAKES ABOUT ½ GALLON

½ gallon apple cider
1 12-ounce can tamarind juice (see Note)

Heat the cider and tamarind juice together in a large saucepan just until it comes to a boil. Serve hot.

NOTE: Tamarind juice, produced by Goya, is sold in major supermarkets.

Banana-Almond Smoothie

This smoothie is a great solution to the age-old dilemma of a bunch of bananas turning black. It's a welcome addition to any breakfast.

MAKES ABOUT 4½ CUPS

3 cups milk, soy milk, or rice milk
3 bananas
1 teaspoon almond extract

Place all the ingredients in a food processor or blender and puree until smooth. Serve.

CHANTING

The morning chanting service at the monastery is delightful, not only because of the rich combination of sound, ritual, and silence, but also because it clears and opens up the diaphragm for the succeeding period of zazen and just makes you feel good. There's something about the harmonious (or sometimes disharmonious) blending of all our voices raised in song that is a perfect beginning to each day. The morning service lasts about one hour, during which the dark of night gradually turns into the light of early morning. The *kanzeon* chant, which is the twelfth of fourteen chants and dedications, is a favorite. The lights are turned off, and the chant is repeated twenty-one times. It builds from slow and quiet to fast and loud. It's followed by a long shout of MU-U-U-U-U-u-u-u-u, then a short but intense period of silence.

The contrast of the quiet with the chanting, the bells, the gongs, and the drums is almost shocking. Our breath surfs on the waves of silence, becoming immersed in it. We, who were moments before linked by our loud chanting, are now connected by each pure breath that we take in the midst of the powerful and thick silence enveloping us all. The birds cooperate for a moment and seem to halt their song. Then their song resumes, and we hear it as never before. The sound of the wind, the rain, even the creaking of the monastery, become distinct. Wind, rain, creaking. It's tempting to sit in this moment forever. But then the tap of the gong recalls us, and we continue with our chanting. We repeat the chanting the next morning and the next and the next. Each morning is different, each sound, each silent moment new. We move through our lives this way. Our lives are movement.

—Myochi

SOME ZEN TERMS

Bodhisattva   An enlightened being filled with wisdom and compassion who is dedicated to helping others attain enlightenment.

Dharma   Immutable, universal truths or cosmic laws upon which Buddha's teachings are based.

Dokusan   A private interview with a teacher to discuss one's meditation practice.

Gassho   A gesture that literally means "palms together"; used often to express reverence and gratitude.

Jihatsu   A set of three stacked bowls used for all formal meals in the monastery.

Jikijitsu   A monk or nun who sits at the head of the zendo and regulates the atmosphere with discipline, encouragement, and his or her own strong example.

Jisha   A monk or nun responsible for the care and comfort of the residents and guests of the monastery.

Kessei   A three-month monastery training program for Zen students.

Kinhin   Walking meditation practiced in between sitting periods.

Koan   An enigmatic Zen story assigned to students to help them come to an intuitive rather than a conceptual understanding of reality.

Rinzai   One of the two main schools of Zen Buddhism, the other being Soto Zen. Rinzai Zen's focus is on koan study, while Soto Zen emphasizes "just sitting."

Samadhi   Deep calmness of mind that is often the result of sitting meditation; a state that can lead to peaceful equanimity.

Sangha   A community of Buddhist practitioners. One of the three treasures of Buddhism, along with Buddha and dharma.

Sarei   A formal tea ceremony that takes place in the zendo twice a day during sesshin.

Sesshin   An intensive, silent meditation retreat lasting from two to eight days.

Teisho   A formal talk given once a day during sesshin by the Zen master. Though not a teaching in the usual sense, this "presentation" by the roshi will often focus on a koan or other Zen story.

Tenzo   The head cook in a monastery; also the kitchen itself.

Zazen   Literally, sitting Zen. This is the core of Zen practice and involves sitting on a cushion and concentrating on one's breath or on a koan. It can lead to great insight and enlightenment.

Zen   Inherently difficult to grasp, Zen is neither philosophy nor religion, but a spiritual system that points us to our inner being and the truth that resides there. Zen holds that nothing need be done, because each one of us at *this* moment is already fully realized. The realization of this truth and the recovery of our true nature lead to ultimate freedom and absolute peace of mind.

Zendo   Literally, "Zen hall." A room in the monastery where zazen is practiced.

GUIDE TO INGREDIENTS

Adzuki, also spelled azuki (ah-ZOO-kee): These small, mahogany-colored beans with a slightly sweet, nutty flavor are grown extensively in China and Japan. They are relatively quick to cook (about 35 minutes after soaking) and are the easiest of all beans to digest. In Japan, they are frequently made into sweets. Adzuki beans are available at Asian markets and some natural food stores.

Arborio rice (ar-BOH-ree-oh): This Italian-grown rice is very high in starch and is shorter and fatter than any other variety of rice. Most commonly used for risotto, it can be found in most large supermarkets and gourmet specialty food stores.

Asiago cheese (ah-see-AH-goh): Made in the Italian province of Vicenza, this cheese is named after the plateau of Asiago, its original production zone. It has a medium-tangy, mellow, yet pronounced flavor that is best described as a cross between Swiss cheese and Parmesan. It is a medium-fat cheese (about 25 percent) produced from partially skimmed cow's milk. Asiago can be found in most large supermarkets and gourmet specialty food stores.

Balsamic vinegar (bal-SAH-mihk): The finest balsamic vinegars are from Modena, where they are aged ten to fifty years in a series of barrels made from different resinous woods, which give them their unique flavor. In a class by itself, balsamic vinegar lacks the sharp taste usually associated with other vinegars. Its flavor is a balance of contrasts: sweet and sharp, spicy and mellow. There is no substitute. Balsamic vinegar should be stored in a cool, dark place. It will lose its flavor in the refrigerator. It should keep for a long time this way but may develop some sediment, which is nothing to worry about. While balsamic vinegar makes a magnificent vinaigrette, it may find its best expression in unlikely roles for vinegar — such as splashed on fresh fruit, fine cheese, or ice cream. It can be drizzled on potatoes, stir-fries, bean or vegetable soups, or grilled vegetables. It can be found in most supermarkets and gourmet specialty food stores.

Barley: The most nutritious form of this hearty grain is hulled barley, which has only the outer husk removed. It is a nutritionally balanced food, high in protein and carbohydrates. It also provides bulk by absorbing two to three times its volume in cooking liquid. Cooked barley can be used in soups, stews, and hot or cold mixed-grain dishes. It is most pleasing when used as a complementary ingredient, not as a main grain. It can be purchased in natural food stores.

Basmati rice (bahs-MAH-tee): This fragrant long-grain rice, with a nutty aroma and almost buttery flavor, is grown in India, Pakistan, and the Middle East. It is more delicate and lower in starch than other long-grain rices and cooks up light and fluffy. It comes in white and brown varieties and can be found in some supermarkets, Indian and Middle Eastern markets, and gourmet specialty food stores.

Bulgur (BUHL-guhr): Nutty flavored with a tender, chewy texture, bulgur is a type of wheat that has been steamed whole, then dried and cracked into grits. Because it is precooked, it is quick and easy to prepare. Bulgur can be found in some supermarkets, Middle Eastern markets, and natural food stores.

Burdock root: A long, slender root vegetable with a rusty brown skin and grayish white flesh, cultivated primarily in Japan, burdock has a fibrous stalk with a sweet flavor and a tender, crisp texture. It is highly prized by the Japanese for its healing properties, for it is said to stimulate circulation and prevent colon cancer. Burdock turns dark quickly when sliced, so it should be placed in water immediately. Thinly slice or grate for use in soups, vegetable, and grain dishes. It can be found in Japanese and Asian markets.

Capers: Small, sun-dried flower buds of the caper bush, native to the Middle East and parts of Asia, these are pickled in salt or a vinegar brine. Rinse well before using. Their piquant flavor goes well with salads or hors d'oeuvres. Capers can be found in most large supermarkets and gourmet specialty food stores.

Chipotle peppers (chi-POHT-lay): These smoked jalapeños lend a smoky, meaty, and spicy essence to dishes. Chipotles can be purchased ground or whole. They can be found in gourmet specialty food stores and are also available from most spice distributors.

Coconut milk: This thick, creamy milk is made from dried coconut flesh, which is soaked and then pressed. Unsweetened canned coconut milk is usually imported from Thailand and is the variety required for cooking. The sweetened varieties are used for frozen drinks. Coconut milk can be purchased in Asian markets and some large supermarkets.

Curry powder: A spice blend, curry powder most commonly consists of cumin, coriander, fenugreek, chili peppers, peppercorns, cinnamon, cloves, cardamom, and turmeric. Many combinations of dried and ground spices can be used. Other spices that can be found in commercial curry powders include ginger, basil, mint, lemongrass, fennel, mustard seeds, and saffron. Curry powder is widely available in supermarkets, gourmet specialty food stores, and Indian and Asian markets.

Daikon (DI-kon): This large, white radish, 12 to 20 inches in length and 2 to 4 inches in diameter, is Japan's most fundamental vegetable. Its flavor is similar to that of a red radish when eaten raw; however, it becomes stronger and turniplike when cooked. Daikon is thought to aid in digesting anything oily. Serve raw in salads, cooked in soups or stews, or steamed or boiled with white miso. Daikon is found in large supermarkets and in Japanese and Asian markets.

Galangal root (guh-LANG-guhl): Cream-colored and closely resembling ginger in both taste and form, galangal differs from ginger in its unique menthol-like aroma and more delicate, almost lemon-lime flavor. Look for it fresh, dried, and frozen in Asian markets. I prefer whole frozen galangal, finding it easiest to grate. Its skin is tender enough that it's not necessary to peel before grating.

Ginger: A very fibrous, cream-colored rhizome (underground stem) with a clean, hot, pungent, and refreshing flavor, ginger goes wonderfully with garlic. It is one of the few ingredients common to all Asian cuisines. Some of the finest ginger is grown in Hawaii. Only fresh ginger is used in Asian cooking, with the powdered form favored for baking. Powdered (ground) ginger cannot replace fresh. Fresh ginger is thought to aid digestion, calm nausea, fight colds, and stimulate the appetite. It can be stored in the refrigerator for a few weeks or frozen, wrapped in plastic, for longer periods. Ginger must be peeled before using because the skin is fibrous. Fresh ginger can be found in most supermarkets, in Asian markets, and in gourmet specialty food stores. Choose stems that are firm and tight, not wrinkled and soft.

Several varieties of pickled ginger can be found in Asian markets. The usually pale pink, thinly sliced type is the best variety to use in recipes that call for pickled ginger. The bright red, julienned pickled ginger has quite a bite to it, but it makes a striking garnish.

Graham flour: This coarsely ground whole wheat flour provides a full wheaty flavor and aroma. It is named after Dr. Sylvester Graham, of graham cracker fame, one of the first modern individuals to promote a vegetarian diet. Sometimes graham flour is labeled "coarse wheat flour." It can be found in natural food stores and some large supermarkets.

Green Thai curry paste: A prepared paste with a base of green chili peppers, which contributes the distinctive green color, green curry paste may include a variety of spices and seasonings, among them galangal, fennel, shallots, garlic, ginger, lemongrass, cloves, cumin, coriander, peppercorns, kaffir lime leaves, and coconut milk. Green Thai curry paste will last for up to two months in the refrigerator and longer in the freezer. It can be purchased in some supermarkets, Asian markets, and gourmet specialty food stores.

Hijiki (hee-JEE-kee): This nutritious, black sea vegetable is high in iron and calcium and also contains protein, vitamins A and B, and trace minerals. Hijiki has a unique, rich, almost nutty flavor. Its short, jagged, spaghettilike strands are more delicate in texture than most seaweed. Sold in dried form, hijiki can easily be reconstituted in water or apple juice (which takes the edge off its flavor) and used as a vegetable in soups, sautés, stir-fries, and salads. It is widely available in Asian markets and natural food stores.

Hoisin sauce (HOY-sihn), also called Peking sauce: This spicy-sweet, brownish red sauce is made from soybeans, sugar, garlic, chilies, and various spices. Thick, with a concentrated flavor, it is usually diluted with water, stock, or sesame oil. Hoisin sauce is usually served as a table condiment, but it can be mixed into many dishes. It can be purchased in supermarkets and Asian markets.

Kaffir lime leaves: Although native to Southeast Asia and Hawaii, the kaffir lime tree is starting to appear in Florida and California. The dark, glossy leaves of the tree have a unique double shape, appearing as two leaves joined end to end. They have an intense citrus aroma and flavor, and they're used much like bay leaves in Thai curries and stews. They can be ripped in half and later removed from a dish or stemmed and finely shredded and left in. A new method that I have discovered is to grind the leaves to a powder in an electric spice grinder. Kaffir lime leaves can be found in the frozen food section of some Asian markets. Store in the freezer.

Kalamata olives (kahl-uh-MAH-tuh): Native to Greece, these almond-shaped, dark purple olives have an intense, rich, and fruity flavor. They can be found in supermarkets as well as in gourmet specialty food stores. They are most economically purchased in small portions from large display barrels.

Kimchee (KIHM-chee): A very hot and pungent pickled and fermented cabbage or other vegetable, kimchee is served as a condiment. It is favored by Koreans. It can be purchased in Korean markets and some Asian and Japanese markets.

Kombu (KOHM-boo): A thick, dark, wide-leafed sea vegetable, kombu is harvested by hand, folded into strips, and dried. It should be gently wiped with a wet cloth before using, but not washed. A staple in Japanese kitchens, it is used for dashi, or stock, and is a good source of calcium and potassium. Beans cooked with a small strip of kombu are said to produce less gas. Kombu can be found in natural food stores and Asian markets.

Kudzu (KOOD-zoo), also spelled kuzu: The tuberous root of kudzu, a plant in the legume family, is dehydrated and pulverized into powder or chunks. This powder is used for thickening sauces, soups, stews, and puddings. Kudzu is high in protein and vitamins A and D. It can be purchased in Asian markets and some natural food stores.

Lemon oil: This pure, potent citrus oil is cold-pressed from lemon rind. It can be found in gourmet specialty food stores or mail-ordered from Boyajian (see Mail-Order Sources, page 243). There is no substitute.

Millet: This tiny, round, yellow grain, bland in flavor and rich in protein, is a staple for about one-third of the world's population. It is prepared like rice and used in soups and stews or as a side dish. Millet can be purchased in natural food stores.

Mirin (MIHR-ihn), also called rice wine: This sweet, syrupy cooking wine made from glutinous rice is essential to Japanese cooking. A syrup of one part sugar dissolved in one part water can be substituted. Mirin can be found in all Japanese markets, some Asian markets, some large supermarkets, and some gourmet specialty food stores.

Miso (MEE-soh): An aged soybean paste, rich in protein and B vitamins, ranging in color from cream to reddish brown and in texture from smooth to chunky, miso varies widely in taste and strength, depending on the variety and length of fermentation. White is the sweetest and mildest, with the darker colors having a heartier, saltier flavor. I prefer a combination of the two for most miso soups. There are many brands. Sample a few before choosing a light and a dark favorite. South River Miso Company (see Mail-Order Sources, page 243) has the finest miso I've ever tasted. Because it is expensive, save it for spreads and sauces, where its flavor will be most noticeable. Miso contains organisms that produce enzymes known to aid digestion. It should be added to dishes at the end of the cooking time so as not to destroy the healthful organisms. Boiling not only kills the organisms but also alters its flavor. Used for soups, sauces, and dressings, miso can be found in natural food stores and Japanese and Asian markets.

Nori (NOH-ree): Dark, paper-thin, 7-x-8-inch sheets of dried seaweed with a sweet flavor, nori is used for sushi and thinly sliced as a condiment and garnish for some Japanese foods. It is rich in protein, vitamin A, calcium, iron, and other minerals. Store in an airtight container. Nori can be purchased in natural food stores and Japanese and Asian markets.

Quinoa (KEEN-wah): Though technically the seed of a vegetable and not a true grain, quinoa is used as a grain because of its cooking characteristics. Tiny and bead-shaped, with a delicate, bland flavor, quinoa expands to four times its original volume when cooked. Primarily imported from South and Central America, it has a high protein value, complete with all eight essential amino acids. Quinoa has a natural, bitter coating that is removed commercially. Before cooking, it must be thoroughly rinsed to remove any remaining bits of the coating. Quinoa is used like rice and can be purchased in any natural food store.

Rice vinegar: Made from fermented rice, rice vinegar is slightly milder than most Western vinegars and is a staple in Japanese cooking. It can be found in Japanese and Asian markets and some supermarkets.

Sake (SAH-kee): Potent and slightly sweet, this Japanese rice wine is used for sauces, vegetables, and dashi. The varieties marketed for cooking are cheaper than those for drinking. It is available at Japanese markets and most large liquor stores.

Shiitake mushrooms (shee-TAH-kay), also called Chinese black mushrooms and forest mushrooms: With dark caps that measure 1 to 3 inches in diameter, these mushrooms have a full-bodied, rich, meaty flavor. They are a staple in Asian cooking and the key to a good vegetarian broth. Though the stems are tough and should be removed before eating, they are great for stocks and sauces. Shiitake mushrooms can be purchased both dried and fresh. I prefer the dried variety found in Asian markets. Their quality is superior to American-grown ones, and they are usually cheaper than the ones in supermarkets, gourmet specialty food stores, and natural food stores.

Soba (SOH-buh): These thin, delicate Japanese noodles are made from buckwheat flour or a mixture of buckwheat and wheat flours. There are many brands. Quality and price vary considerably; sample a few before settling on a favorite. Those found in Japanese and Asian markets are considerably cheaper than those sold in natural food stores.

Soy flour: Made from finely ground roasted soybeans, with a slightly nutty flavor, this flour adds a pleasant texture and flavor to many foods. It's low in carbohydrates, extremely rich in high-quality protein, and an excellent source of iron, calcium, and B vitamins. Soy flour can be used to thicken gravies or sauces, and in baking it can replace up to one-fourth of the total flour called for in a recipe (it has no gluten). Soy flour is sold in natural food stores and some supermarkets.

Spices and herbs: Fresh spices and herbs are essential to flavorful food. They should be stored in a cool, dry place away from the stove, oven, or other appliances that generate heat, which will weaken their flavor. Dampness can cause clumping and caking. Exposure to bright light or oxygen will also damage them. While whole spices will last for three to four years, ground spices are at their optimum strength for only six months to one year. To determine if a particular spice or herb is fresh, look for

fading of color, loss of aroma when crushed between your fingers, and, though it may seem obvious, taste. If it tastes like dust or has a substantial loss of color or a minimal aroma, replace it. If possible, purchase spices in whole form and grind them as needed in an electric coffee grinder reserved for that purpose.

Tahini (tah-HEE-nee), also called sesame butter: A paste made from ground raw or toasted sesame seeds, tahini has a smooth, creamy texture, is high in fat and protein, and is rich in calcium. Traditionally used in Middle Eastern cooking in such dishes as hummus and baba ghanoush, it has become a staple of the American vegetarian scene. Tahini is sold in Middle Eastern markets, some supermarkets, gourmet specialty food stores, and natural food stores.

Takuan (TAH-kwan): Bright yellow, crunchy, odiferous, and pungent, this pickled daikon is a good condiment for simple rice dishes. It can be purchased in Japanese and Asian markets.

Tamari (tah-MAH-ree): This dark sauce made from fermented soybeans is similar to soy sauce, but thicker, with a richer, finer taste. I use it in place of or in addition to salt to add depth to a dish. It can be purchased in natural food stores but is less expensive in Japanese and Asian markets.

Tamarind (TAM-uh-rind), also called Indian date: The fruit of a shade tree that grows in Asia, northern Africa, and India, tamarind is popular as a flavoring in East India and the Middle East. It can be found in East Indian and some Asian markets in various forms: jars of syrup or pulp, cans of paste, or whole tamarind pods dried into blocks or ground into powder.

Tempeh (TEHM-pay): A fermented soybean cake with a chewy, meaty texture, a mushroomlike aroma, and a complex, almost nutty flavor, tempeh is high in protein and low in saturated fat. It's also a good source of iron, calcium, and B vitamins. Popular in Asian and vegetarian cooking, it can be purchased in large supermarkets and natural food stores.

Tofu (TOH-foo): High in protein and minerals, easy to digest, and low in saturated fat, this soy wonder food is used extensively in vegetarian and Asian cuisines. It is made of soy milk coagulated to form curds, through a process similar to that used to transform milk into cheese. Tofu's chameleonlike nature allows it to take on any flavor. It can be steamed, stewed, broiled, baked, grilled, roasted, served raw, used in soups, stir-fries, and casseroles, or blended into many kinds of dressings and toppings. Tofu comes in various textures, from soft and silky to dense and chewy. Frozen, it takes on the spongy texture of meat. I keep a few pounds of tofu in the freezer so they are always on hand when I need them. For freezing and thawing information, see page 65. Packaged tofu can be purchased in large supermarkets, Japanese and Asian markets, and natural food stores, while fresh tofu is found only in some Asian markets and natural food stores.

Keep fresh tofu refrigerated, covered with water (which should be changed daily), for up to one week.

Udon (oo-DOHN): These thick, squared or rounded white noodles are usually made from wheat flour, salt, and water. A national favorite in Japan, they are eaten al dente with broth or dashi. Udon noodles are available in Japanese and Asian markets and natural food stores.

Umeboshi plums (oo-meh-BOH-she): Commonly referred to as "pickled Japanese plums," umeboshi are actually a type of apricot. Picked before ripening, they are then alternately soaked in brine and red shiso leaves (which gives them their characteristic deep pink color) and sun-dried many times. Because they have a salty and tart flavor, umeboshi plums are an apt accompaniment to many Japanese meals. Umeboshi paste, made from pureed plums, is a popular seasoning in Japan. Stocked in every Japanese household, umeboshi plums are said to have many medicinal qualities, including aiding digestion and purifying the blood. They can be purchased in all Japanese and some Asian markets and in some natural food stores.

Wakame (wah-KAH-meh): In its dried form, wakame looks like hard black curls or wood shavings. Once it has been reconstituted, it turns deep green and takes on a delicate texture, powerful presence, and rich flavor. Rinse and soak wakame for about 20 minutes in tepid water. It has a tough spine that may need to be cut away if it has not already been removed. Wakame is high in iron and calcium. To prevent the loss of nutrients, do not cook it for more than one minute. Wakame is used in soups, salads, and simmered dishes. It can be found in Japanese and Asian markets and some natural food stores.

Wasabi (WAH-sah-bee): Although it's often called Japanese horseradish, wasabi is not related to horseradish. A bright green, sharp, and fiery condiment that is traditionally served with sushi and sashimi, wasabi comes in paste and powder forms. It's available in Japanese and Asian markets and some natural food stores.

Whole wheat pastry flour: This finely textured flour milled from soft wheat has less gluten and therefore less protein than regular whole wheat flour. It gives muffins and quick breads a tenderer crumb but is not suitable for yeast breads, which need a higher gluten content.

MAIL-ORDER SOURCES

Boyajian, Inc.
349 Lennox Street
Norwood, MA 02062
781-440-9500

Manufactures pure citrus oil and other flavoring oils.

Lee Valley Tools
P.O. Box 1780
Ogdensburg, NY 13669-6780
800-871-8158

Sells the Microplane Zester, a miracle citrus zester and hard cheese grater that has become indispensable in my kitchen. This grater works well for fresh ginger and frozen galangal. Designed like a woodworker's rasp but with a handle, it produces delicate, snowflakelike gratings that don't get trapped in the holes as they do in a box grater.
   Product/Model #: 27W0410
   Price: About $11.00, plus tax, shipping, and handling.

South River Miso Company
South River Farm
Conway, MA 01341
413-369-4057

The only unpasteurized, certified organic miso available, handcrafted in the centuries-old farmhouse tradition. The motto on the brochure reads: "A gift from the Gods." If you are a connoisseur or even if you are just discovering miso, try South River's. The company makes ten different varieties and sells sampler packages.

FORM

INDEX